Backyards

A *Sunset* Design Guide

by Bridget Biscotti Bradley and the editors of Sunset Books

Contents

Creating a backyard that's comfortable and enjoyable will make your home feel exponentially larger. Just think of being able to invite friends and family over for a weekend pool party or summer barbecue, where guests can mingle indoors and out. This book will guide you through the process of turning backyard dreams into reality. Learn how to make the most of small spaces, incorporate the needs of children and pets, and add structures that give even nondescript homes a sense of style. You'll also find advice on using eco-friendly materials and planning water-wise gardens.

Throughout the book, you'll find words of wisdom from our panel of experts, as well as case studies of their work that will inspire you with possibilities for your own backyard.

SUNSET BOOKS
Vice President, Editorial Director: Bob Doyle
Art Director: Vasken Guiragossian

STAFF FOR THIS BOOK
Senior Editor: Carrie Dodson Davis
Project Editor: Terri L. Robertson
Consulting Editor: Marianne Lipanovich
Principal Photographer: Michele Lee Willson
Principal Photo Stylist: Laura Del Fava
Copy Editor: John Edmonds
Proofreader: Denise Griffiths
Indexer: Marjorie Joy
Prepress Coordinators: Danielle Johnson and
Eligio Hernandez
Production: Precision Graphics
Intern: Shea Staskowski

Cover Photo: Photography by
Steven A. Gunther.
Design by Judy Kameon,
Elysian Landscapes.

10 9 8 7 6 5 4 3 2 1
First Printing January 2009

For additional copies of
Backyards: A Sunset Design Guide
or any other Sunset book,
visit us at www.oxmoorhouse.com.
For more exciting home and garden ideas,
visit www.myhomeideas.com

Design Panel

The following design and building professionals from across the United States lent their enormous talent and valuable advice to the pages of this book.

Brian Koch
LANDSCAPE CONTRACTOR

W. Brian Koch is the owner of Terra Ferma Landscapes Inc., a landscape design-build company located in the San Francisco Bay Area. He earned an Ornamental Horticulture degree from University of Vermont and his Certificate for Landscape Architecture through UC Berkeley Extension. Combining practical construction knowledge and innovative creative abilities, Brian has designed and crafted many unique and functional residential landscape spaces and gardens.
www.tflandscapes.com

William Morrow
LANDSCAPE DESIGNER

William Morrow was born and raised in Washington DC and attended Texas A&M University. After a career in environmental protection, he opened William Morrow Garden Design in Georgetown, specializing in urban gardens. William's philosophy is that a garden is a sum of its parts, and as a whole creates a mood or a feeling for a space.
www.morrowgardendesign.com

Patricia St. John
LANDSCAPE DESIGNER

Patricia St. John has been designing gardens for the last 11 years through her company, St. John Landscapes. She is a Certified Professional Landscape Designer and California Certified Nursery Professional, and teaches in the Landscape Horticulture department at Merritt College in Oakland. Patricia loves creating gardens that have an abundance of color, texture, and year-round interest, where environmentally conscious decisions for design, plants, and materials can be made. Patricia lives in Berkeley, California, with her husband, Martin.
www.stjohnlandscapes.com

Ken Coverdell
LANDSCAPE ARCHITECT AND CONTRACTOR

Ken Coverdell is a licensed landscape contractor, landscape architect, and general contractor. As a horticulturist, soil expert, and water conservationist, he has grown Blue Sky Designs, Inc., from a two-person team to a full-service operation with more than 30 employees. The landscape designers and crews are experienced at designing and building everything from hilltop pools and luxurious spas with detailed masonry to lush gardens that incorporate the client's dreams, imagination, and desire to be surrounded by beauty.
www.blueskydesignsinc.com

Katey Mulligan
LANDSCAPE DESIGNER

Katey Mulligan is an award-winning landscape designer and recipient of Sunset's Western Living Award at the 2006 San Francisco Flower and Garden Show. Through her business, Liquidambar Garden Design, Katey specializes in transforming ordinary or difficult sites into gardens that blend function and aesthetics. A native of Dublin, Ireland, she was educated in Ireland, England, and the United States. Katey's international exposure through education and extensive world travel informs her broad cultural and environmental perspective.
www.liquidambar.biz

Craig Bergmann
LANDSCAPE ARCHITECT

Craig Bergmann Landscape Design (CBLD) was founded in 1986 and has four divisions: Design, Installation, Garden Care, and Nursery. Craig serves as Head of Design, working with a staff of 75 employees, including six designers. He is a registered Landscape Architect and frequent lecturer, and was recently featured as a nationwide speaker in *Horticulture* magazine's Nationwide Symposia Series. CBLD is noted for its modern-day twists on the romantic designs of the past, and the company has received numerous awards, including Best of Show at several consecutive Chicago Flower & Garden Shows.
www.craigbergmann.com

Rob Pressman
LANDSCAPE ARCHITECT

Over the course of his 35-year career in landscape architecture, Rob Pressman has worked on five continents, designing a wide range of thoughtful, site-specific projects in Los Angeles and Jerusalem, Shanghai and Shenzhen, Melbourne and Monrovia (Liberia). He has a Bachelor of Science degree in the conservation of natural resources from the University of California, Berkeley, and a Master of Landscape Architecture degree from Harvard Graduate School of Design. Rob currently runs TGP, Inc., with landscape architect Marianne Liggett in Encino, California, where they focus on high-density, multifamily residential and mixed-use projects.
www.tgpinc.net

Kelly Bowman Greenwood
LANDSCAPE DESIGNER

Kelly Bowman Greenwood believes that kids and pets are part of the fun in a landscape, not simply challenges to overcome. A graduate of Sweet Briar College, she received a Certificate in Landscape Design from the University of California, Berkeley. Kelly lives with her husband, daughter, and perpetually evolving garden amid the redwoods near Pescadero, California.
www.greenwoodlandscape.com

Chapter 1
Getting Started

Perhaps you've just moved into a new house without any landscaping and need to turn a blank slate into something usable for your family. Or maybe you've lived in a house for years and are finally able to spend some money redesigning the backyard. Whatever your situation, your first task is the same: to determine how to make your backyard a place you want to spend time in. There is no right answer or one-size-fits-all design. This chapter will get you thinking about how your backyard can function better for you and your family.

Creating Outdoor Spaces

A decorative gate leading to the backyard gives visitors the feeling that they're about to see something special.

Inside the house, you have rooms dedicated to specific tasks and the activities that take place throughout the day. A well-designed backyard should function in much the same way. Think about how you can create defined areas for relaxation, play, exercise, storage, entertaining, dining, and any other activity that is a regular part of your life.

Assessing the Landscape

With notebook and pen in hand, walk through your garden. Jot down what areas are shady, sunny, windy, pleasant smelling, or private. What areas are visible to your neighbors? Is there any noise coming from nearby homes or traffic? Where are the existing mature trees that you need to work the new design around? Take a folding chair out and sit for a few minutes in the areas you're considering for dining or lounging to see how the area feels or what could make it more comfortable. Don't forget to look at the side yards as well and note any problems that need to be remedied, such as storage or an abundance or lack of plants.

Then go inside the house and look out at the garden from each room. Notice any views that you'd like to block with plants, or stretches of open fencing that make the backyard look plain.

Are there any existing plants that hide the view of an area you need to see from indoors, such as a play area for children?

Walk out of each door that leads from the house to the backyard and think about which direction you naturally want to meander in. Do you envision lots of curved paths, straight lines outlining patios, or a combination of both? Does your personal style or the style of your home intimate a more formal or casual design? This question applies not only to hardscaping elements like paths and decks but also to overhead structures, furniture, and plants.

LEFT If the best spot for dining also gets direct sun when you want to be outside, incorporate an umbrella into your outdoor table.

BELOW LEFT A concrete patio and white walls serve as a blank canvas for a succulent garden in various shades of green.

BELOW Evenly spaced concrete stepping-stones combined with concrete spheres add graphic appeal to a narrow side yard.

RIGHT There's a fluid feeling in this backyard, thanks to a low, curved wall that frames a lush planting bed combined with diagonal pavers.

Listing Your Goals

Now is the time to decide what you want out of your backyard remodel. The reasons that follow are among the most common for undertaking a landscape project, and should give you some ideas and help ensure that you cover your bases.

PRIVACY can be a luxury in some areas and taken for granted where houses are spread far apart. People tend to spend more time in backyards that feel private and hidden from view.

ENTERTAINING outdoors opens up many more possibilities for at-home events than if you had to keep guests inside. If you are designing a backyard for entertaining, incorporate a large deck or patio and multiple seating areas, and think about adding a swimming pool and an outdoor kitchen.

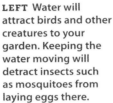

LEFT Water will attract birds and other creatures to your garden. Keeping the water moving will detract insects such as mosquitoes from laying eggs there.

RIGHT An iron fence separates this vegetable patch from the rest of the garden, and it helps keep some animals out.

GROWING your own herbs, fruits, and vegetables is a rewarding hobby and teaches children valuable lessons about where food comes from. The popularity of eating organic and local has resulted in more people deciding to grow food in their backyards. Kitchen gardens need to be placed in a part of the yard that gets plenty of sun. If you also want to compost, plan now for how you will hide that area from view when you're looking out at the garden from the house.

ANIMAL AND INSECT lovers may want to attract birds, butterflies, and other wildlife to the garden. Incorporate plants and small water features that these creatures are drawn to, and place them near the windows of the house if you want to watch the action from indoors.

MODIFYING THE CLIMATE around your home can be an intentional goal or an added benefit of your remodel. Plant new deciduous trees that will shade the house in summer and allow the sun to reach the house when the leaves fall off in winter. Build walls or fences that block prevailing winds.

SAVING WATER is a crucial issue that most everyone needs to improve upon and make a high priority when remodeling the backyard. Remove as much existing lawn as possible, don't add any new lawn, use native and low-water plants, and plan your irrigation system wisely to reduce runoff and overspray. Consider incorporating a rainwater collection container in your design that can be used to irrigate the landscape.

EXERCISING at home by swimming or playing sports is a great way to stay in shape. Recreation areas for activities like these, as well as children's play spaces, need to be carefully incorporated into the landscape so that they don't overwhelm the design.

LEFT This stream, planted with aquatic iris, attracts birds, dragonflies, and frogs to the backyard.

TOP Almost as important as having a large space for entertaining is how you access the backyard from the house. In this relatively simple backyard, two sets of double doors lead out to a small patio that borders the swimming pool.

ABOVE LEFT Water-wise choices include using native plants and hardscaping instead of grass. Here, crushed stone from a local quarry surrounds a California pepper tree.

ABOVE RIGHT Seating areas in both shade and sun allow swimmers a choice of where to relax poolside.

LEFT Large trees create a sense of privacy in this colorful courtyard, where visitors can either sip drinks on the plush outdoor furniture or step down into the inviting spa for a soak.

ABOVE These stucco walls keep large gusts of wind at bay but allow some air to flow through spaces in the terra-cotta roof tiles interspersed within the wall.

Defining Separate Rooms

Once you have a list of activities you want to accommodate in your new backyard, think about how to define each area. The idea is to create cozy retreats or spaces for particular activities throughout the garden in a subtle way that creates a unified look but also clearly guides foot traffic.

Use hardscaping elements to define spaces. For example, you may use the same stone for paths and patios, but changing the pattern at each activity area will signal that you have arrived at a destination point. Low stone walls surrounding a dining area will set it apart from the rest of the garden, much as a trellis that you walk under can announce that you've entered the veggie patch. A freestanding pergola creates a quiet space for reading or meditation.

"When the topography allows, terracing is a wonderful way to separate spaces into discrete rooms," explains landscape designer William Morrow. "Even a single step can create a sense of transition, of leaving one space and entering another."

Plants are often used to add a sense of privacy or mystery to certain areas of the garden. Place a row of tall potted plants along the side of the patio that is visible to your neighbor. Or have climbing vines grow along a wall, serving as a backdrop for a pair of lounge chairs. Children love to play hide-and-seek among the shrubbery, whether the plantings are growing free and wild or arranged into neat mazelike hedges. Lawns or layers of mulch surrounding climbing equipment can also define play areas.

LANDSCAPE DESIGNER WILLIAM MORROW ON

Rooms Without Walls

If you look at how most houses are designed today, the singular 'great room' floor plan dominates modern living. With this approach, furnishings are used to delineate a space into different functions—or rooms without walls, as I like to call them. Similarly, in the backyard, careful placement of a trio of large, 3-foot-tall planters can serve as a screen and divide up a large space."

TOP When you have an outdoor area with a solid roof, consider using upholstered furniture and light fixtures that would normally be seen indoors.

OPPOSITE PAGE, TOP LEFT Even in a small courtyard it's possible to create a space just for kids.

OPPOSITE PAGE, TOP RIGHT Children love to play around this circular hedge with a spray fountain in the center.

RIGHT Raised planters surround this seating area, separating it from the dining area beyond.

Oversized furniture, throw pillows, and porcelain teacups give this cabana the look of an upscale indoor drawing room. Swaths of outdoor fabric can be tied back to allow views of the garden.

LEFT Tucked into a corner of a small garden that's surrounded by translucent reed fencing is a diminutive garden pool with room for a bench to enjoy it.

ABOVE Drapes are available when the wind or sun makes outdoor dining less pleasant.

TOP If your favorite flowers won't grow in your soil, keep them in pots instead of undertaking a massive effort to amend the ground soil.

LEFT It might not be the traditional place for a vegetable garden, but in this case the side yard gets the most sun, so it made sense to put raised beds up against the house.

RIGHT In a desert climate, choose plants that will thrive in that environment, such as cactus, yellow-flowering palo verde, and agave.

Work with What You Have

It's usually better to embrace Mother Nature than to force her to change. So before you decide to start your backyard design from scratch, try to appreciate the character and topography of the site for what it is and see if there are ways to work what's already there into the design.

Most people have to incorporate existing mature trees into their plans. While it's often a blessing to have large trees on your property because they make the area seem more established and provide summer shade, they can limit your

design options. Deal with large trees as best you can by working in a seating area under their branches. Choose shade-loving plants to put around tree bases, or mulch that allows water to reach their roots.

Plants that are native to your area will do the best in your backyard. Landscape architect Craig Bergmann suggests looking to nature to decide what plants to incorporate. "For example, if you have a boulder in the backyard, choose plants to surround it that usually grow near rocks you happen across in the wild," Bergmann says.

Pay attention to existing drainage conditions in your yard. While problem areas are best dealt with during the construction phase, you may also choose plants that will do well in those spots as they are. For example, a location that tends to get wet and boggy could feature water plants, saving you from having to install drainage.

Designing for Privacy

ABOVE This low stone wall effectively shields the pool from wind and traffic noise, while the waterfall provides a peaceful sound.

Few of us want to be on display when relaxing in the backyard. We'd like to feel as though we're in another room of the house—one with fresh air and sunshine. But before you start planting a fortress of plants, walk around the yard at various times of the day to see which areas need to be protected from sight or sound. Consider sun patterns and any views that you want to preserve.

Blocking Noise

Sounds of nearby traffic can make your backyard feel like less of an oasis from the hustle and bustle of everyday life. Even worse is when close neighbors tend to turn up their stereos or televisions loud enough for you to hear them on a regular basis. Or you may live near a freeway that supplies a constant whir of cars passing by. Moving-water features, such as spill fountains and waterfalls, will mask some noises by giving you something else to listen to. But the best way to block sound is with a solid barrier such as a fence or wall. A tall berm or mound of soil planted with shrubs and trees also buffers sound and gives the backyard a more natural feel.

Fences and Walls

Most backyards have a fence bordering the property line. Take this opportunity to assess the fence's condition and determine whether it needs to be replaced. Perhaps some of the posts have been eaten by termites or worn away from rot. Get a quote for replacing just the rotted or eaten pieces so you can preserve the majority of the fence. New wood likely won't be the same color as aged wood, but those aesthetic differences can be masked with plants. Replacing large amounts of fencing is a surprisingly costly proposition. If you do need to have a new fence installed, consider going higher if you have problems with visibility from neighboring yards.

Walls made of stone, brick, concrete, or stucco are most often used inside the backyard rather than at the property line. Use them to define spaces throughout the garden or to block wind from barreling through dining or seating areas. Some walls may be kept low enough for people to see over, while others can create private hideaways. Low walls should have a wide cap piece so they can serve as seating areas when you entertain.

Gates

Most side yards have a gate that leads to the backyard. Just like the front door to your house, the style of the gate should match what's beyond. Gates can be the same size and material as the surrounding fence, or you can combine mediums, such as putting a wooden gate in a stone wall. The size of the gate sends a message as well: Low gates or those you can see through are welcoming, while high and solid gates say that privacy is a main concern.

Gates should be at least 3 feet wide, but something wider will be more comfortable to pass through and will more easily allow you to take lawn equipment and wheelbarrows from the backyard to the front.

LEFT Layered plantings can disguise sections of a wooden fence that have recently been replaced.

RIGHT TOP Colorful and sculptural plants break up the monotony of a mortared stone wall.

RIGHT BOTTOM This rusted metal fence with a tree-shaped design is brought to life by a climbing vine that stretches across from the hinged side.

Small Yards

Instead of one solid patio, this backyard uses random-sized stepping-stones to make a small space seem bigger.

Though small backyards may seem to limit your options, with smart planning they usually can accommodate several defined spaces and activities. Just as you would for a large backyard, start by deciding how you want to use your garden. Do you envision a quiet place to sit, an area for the kids to play safely, and a section dedicated to growing heirloom tomatoes? Once you work around existing trees and take views and sun patterns into account, you may have to give up something. But a good landscape designer will help you take advantage of every inch and ensure that the design will grow with your family.

One way to add elements without increasing the square footage is to think in terms of what you can do vertically. Use vines, narrow upright trees, raised planters, and pedestals. But don't get carried away, as it's best to leave an open area near the center to maximize the feeling of spaciousness.

Layered plants give small spaces more dimension. Try covering a wall or fence with vines or espaliered trees, then plant a row of shrubs in front of the wall and add ground covers or flowers in front of the shrubs. These layers of greenery will also divert your attention from the periphery of the garden.

Landscape designer Katey Mulligan suggests slightly angling hardscape elements such as pavers and walls to make small spaces feel bigger. This can make a yard seem deeper than it is, and also directs your view away from your neighbor's yard.

ABOVE In a small and narrow yard, this bench and pergola are set at an angle to the house to make the space seem wider. A recirculating fountain at the base of the bench creates a sense of movement.

RIGHT Carve out room for a small-scale waterfall. This one was created with an antique urn turned on its side.

BELOW These low stucco walls provide color, a place to sit, and also an extra planting area for even more color and texture.

LANDSCAPE DESIGNER KATEY MULLIGAN ON

Maximizing Space

When a client wants to pile things on top of each other in a small space, I encourage them to prioritize what they really want and what they can leave out. Another option is considering what elements can be mobile. Everything should have at least two uses in small spaces, and sometimes three. For example, a retaining wall can be used as extra seating and also a table."

LEFT To make the most of this small back porch, a padded cushion was made to turn the low stone wall into a lounging area. A swing hangs from the open side.

ABOVE This small garden was successfully divided into separate rooms for living and dining. Various shades of green plants keep the landscaping simple and allow for furniture to provide bursts of accent color. Mondo grass grows between geometrically placed concrete pavers.

Chapter 2

Backyard Spaces

Backyard hardscaping includes patios, decks, and paths, which define activity areas and lead you from one destination point to the next. The materials you build with will influence the style and function of your outdoor living spaces and will indicate whether your garden is meant to be traveled through efficiently or leisurely. This chapter discusses all of your hardscaping options, including suggestions on giving your garden height and drama with trellises and arbors. It also covers the pros and cons of incorporating a traditional lawn into the backyard when water is increasingly precious.

Patios

A patio just outside the back door serves as a transition between indoor and outdoor spaces, bridging the gap between the protection of the house and the openness of the yard. Patios can also be built in the center or at the edges of the backyard as destination points or to carve out an area for a particular activity, such as dining or lounging by the pool. A low wall can surround all or part of the patio, or you can simply edge the area with the same material used for the patio surface or with a contrasting stone or brick.

Before deciding on patio materials, consider the style and proportions of the house. For example, if it includes brick details, then a brick patio will seem like more of an extension of the structure than a flagstone patio would. Study the house for patterns and details you can mimic on the patio, and look to the window and door dimensions to guide your decisions on scale.

Generally, a 400-square-foot patio is an appropriate size for a small family. If your backyard is large enough, make the patio approximately the size of the adjacent room so

LEFT A wide flagstone patio extends the adjoining living space and allows for a seating area near the garden pool.

ABOVE RIGHT The term "terrace" is often used to describe one or more patios situated on a slope. In this example, a series of flagstone terraces leads up to a gate at the edge of the backyard.

RIGHT Weathered bricks set in a herringbone pattern visually connect with the brick house without mirroring its running bond pattern. Though this patio is small, it has enough room for both a conversation spot and a dining area.

FAR RIGHT A band of river rocks at the edge of this curved patio provides texture and keeps people from walking too close to the plants.

that it feels like you're doubling your living space. Try to line up the patio's edges with a window or door to keep it symmetrical against the house. Your landscape architect or builder will make sure that the patio is graded away from the structure. "The grade should be at least ⅛ inch per foot to ensure that you don't have a problem with standing water, or water making its way into your home," says landscape contractor Brian Koch.

Destination Patios

Building one or more patios farther out in the yard will help you define spaces for particular activities. Work with the existing landscape to carve out these areas so they blend in rather than look as though they were dropped down from the sky. Adding plants around the patio is a great way to soften the edges a bit and provide a natural transition between landscape and hardscape. For the most naturalistic patio, use mulch or gravel and let the patio bleed into the landscape without a hard edge.

LEFT This slate patio puts a side yard to good use as an alternative dining area. The small water feature disguises street noise and creates a relaxing ambiance under the arbor.

BELOW LEFT An elegant stone patio is enveloped by potted plants and topiaries.

BELOW RIGHT A tiered grouping of potted plants works wonders to soften the edge of this patio against the house.

LANDSCAPE DESIGNER
KATEY MULLIGAN ON

Choosing Local Materials

Using local stone sets your garden in context. "For example, in Sonoma County, California, people use a lot of Napa fieldstone or Sonoma wall rock because it's quarried locally, making it less expensive and an eco-friendlier choice. But it also gives the garden a native, aged look."

Nestled in the back corner of a yard under towering redwood trees, this circular patio is surrounded by a low stone wall. The same stone acts as a free-form edging along the grass.

Courtyards

Tucked up against the house and bordered by three or more walls, a courtyard can be a secluded place to sit and relax, or dine and entertain. It can also be a transition between two or more sections of the house. When surrounded by four walls, a courtyard is truly another room of the house, albeit one without a solid roof. Children can play outdoors unattended, and the courtyard can be outfitted with potted plants to bring in color and fragrance.

Separated by large glass doors, this courtyard patio is a seamless extension of the adjoining indoor space and creates an alternative seating area for entertaining. Tall and narrow conifers planted in a narrow trough partially obscure the view of a neighbor. A black iron fence sits low enough to allow a view of the surrounding neighborhood while safely keeping children and pets on the courtyard.

Courtyards in condominium, townhouse, and apartment buildings may be visible to neighbors. Use umbrellas to provide privacy from above, and tall potted plants around the perimeter.

LEFT In housing complexes where courtyards are surrounded by blank walls, adding a climbing vine will make it feel more like a backyard.

BELOW The tall lattice fence around this stone courtyard is covered in foliage, creating a green backdrop for the colorful potted plants below.

RIGHT This breezeway courtyard gets plenty of use as an extra dining area. Because it can be seen from each wing of the house, it feels like a natural extension of indoor living spaces.

LANDSCAPE DESIGNER
KATEY MULLIGAN ON

Making Courtyards Feel Larger

If you choose square-cut stones to pave your courtyard, place them at an angle to the house. "This makes the space feel larger and gives it more movement."

When backyards are sloped or the unevenness of the terrain makes it difficult to build a patio, decks are an ideal solution. Wooden structures can be freestanding or attached to the house, and if you choose composite decking instead of natural wood, you won't have much annual maintenance to do.

Like patios, decks can act as transitions from the home to the backyard, or they can be their own destination. Design the deck to match the style of the house. For example, a white-painted house with no natural wood trim would look best with a painted white deck, while a wood-shingled house would work with a stained deck that uses the same or a complementary wood species.

For a two-story house, a deck extending out from the top floor will give a bird's-eye view of the backyard, but your neighbors will be able to see you more clearly. Work in railings and built-in planters to block views when necessary. Stairs leading from the deck to the backyard can be merely functional, or they can be designed low and wide to serve as extra seating.

LEFT This deck spans two sections of the house and leads down to a guest cottage farther back into the yard. Decorative details, such as using the same wood species for the deck furniture and incorporating orange pots and cushions, make the deck feel more like an outdoor room that's part of the home itself.

ABOVE RIGHT What better way to enjoy a backyard pond than to build a floating deck in the middle of it? The deck's curved edge gives it a soft and natural feel.

RIGHT Cutouts that allow trees or grasses to grow within the deck will help tie it into the rest of the yard.

FAR RIGHT On this deck, a raised planter is nestled between a built-in bench and a set of steps.

Decks for All Purposes

Deck styles range from small and square and sitting on the ground to multilevel affairs with separate seating, dining, and entertaining areas. While the size of the deck depends upon how much of the backyard you want to turn over for this purpose, the shape and the way it connects to the landscape beyond have more to do with the style of your garden and that of the house.

Work curves or uneven edges into the deck to make the surface look as though it washes into the garden. If the deck is a few feet above the ground, add plants around the perimeter to hide the base from view. Decks meant primarily for dining are best built off the kitchen or family room. Consider building an overhead structure for shade, and keep plants that attract bees away from this area. Built-in lighting will allow you to dine alfresco even after the sun goes down.

Decks can also wrap around the house or connect two or more wings. Break up large expanses of decking by allowing nature through in the form of cutouts for existing trees. Pots of flowers or bamboo can add color to the deck and help direct foot traffic.

ABOVE The designer of this deck played with scale by using narrow metal rods for balusters to contrast the wide wooden posts, rails, and stairs.

LEFT Composite decking comes in many colors. Here, the designer made the most of a small space by integrating benches and planters and building steps leading in different directions.

OPPOSITE PAGE A small, low-lying deck that extends out to the water is the perfect spot for a pair of Adirondack chairs.

Choosing Materials

For the structure of your deck, you'll likely need pressure-treated wood, which will last longer outdoors than untreated wood. Environmentally friendly treatment options include wood treated with ammoniacal copper quaternary (ACQ) and copper azole (CA), in which copper is the active ingredient and will prevent the boards from rotting. Look for hardware that won't deteriorate when it comes in contact with ACQ- and CA-treated wood, such as stainless steel.

If you want natural wood, choose one that bears the Forest Stewardship Council (FSC) label, which indicates that the wood was forested responsibly.

Another environmentally friendly choice is composite decking, made of recycled plastic and ground-up waste wood. High-quality composites mimic the grain pattern of natural wood and will stand up well to weather and wear. Unlike natural wood, composite decking doesn't splinter, and some types offer a relatively maintenance-free deck, as they don't need regular sanding and resealing.

LEFT This poured concrete patio was tinted, and then a paper stencil was laid across the surface to create the look of grout lines. A textured roller formed a rippled surface that looks like mortared stone.

ABOVE Terra-cotta–colored Saltillo tiles top a base layer of cement on this patio floor.

RIGHT TOP Regular maintenance is required to keep this Alaska cedar deck looking its best.

RIGHT BOTTOM Slate's rough surface is a good nonslip choice for a patio floor and provides interesting texture on planter boxes.

Hardscaping at a glance

Brick

- **Pros:** Easy to maintain, durable.
- **Cons:** Moss can grow on bricks, making them slippery.
- **Price:** $–$$
- **Installation:** On sand or mortared onto a concrete slab. Choose SX-rated bricks if you live where the ground freezes and thaws.
- **Green Tip:** For a bit more money, you can buy salvaged brick.

Ceramic Tile

- **Pros:** Vast array of colors and shapes.
- **Cons:** Glazed tiles can be slippery when wet.
- **Price:** $–$$
- **Installation:** Be sure to choose tiles rated for your climate and set them in a bed of mortar on top of a concrete slab.
- **Green Tip:** Choose tiles made of recycled materials when possible.

Composite Decking

- **Pros:** Durable, won't splinter, provides excellent traction, resists rotting and insects, and doesn't need to be resealed.
- **Price:** $$$
- **Installation:** Similar to that of wood decking. Some brands use proprietary fastening systems.
- **Green Tip:** Composites are an eco-friendly choice because they are made from sawdust and recycled plastics.

Concrete

- **Pros:** Can be stamped, colored, or decorated with stone or glass; easy to maintain.
- **Cons:** Unless it's textured, it can be slippery when wet.
- **Price:** $$–$$$
- **Installation:** Should be done by a professional with plenty of experience.

- **Green Tip:** Ask your contractor to use recycled fly ash in the mix and to use nontoxic pigments if you're adding color. Permeable poured concrete allows rainwater to seep into the ground rather than run off into the local storm drains, polluting water supplies.

Concrete Pavers

- **Pros:** Widely available in many shapes and colors; easy to replace damaged pavers.
- **Price:** $–$$
- **Installation:** Requires a permanent border to prevent shifting. Pavers are installed over compacted gravel topped with bedding sand.
- **Green Tip:** Permeable pavers allow rainwater to seep into the ground rather than run off into local storm drains, polluting water supplies.

Paving Stones

- **Pros:** These stones are quarried in flat, thin sheets. Irregular flagstones create an informal look, while cut rectangular pieces are more formal.
- **Cons:** Using natural stone requires dealing with differences in height and irregular surfaces, making installation more challenging.
- **Price:** $$–$$$
- **Installation:** Can be laid over a sand base or mortared onto a concrete slab.
- **Green Tip:** Choose paving stones that are quarried locally.

Wood

- **Pros:** A variety of wood species allows for design options; has a natural look.
- **Cons:** Wood requires seasonal maintenance such as sanding and sealing.
- **Price:** $–$$$
- **Installation:** Building a wooden patio is similar to building a deck.
- **Green Tip:** Choose sustainably harvested species and finish with low-VOC stains and sealants.

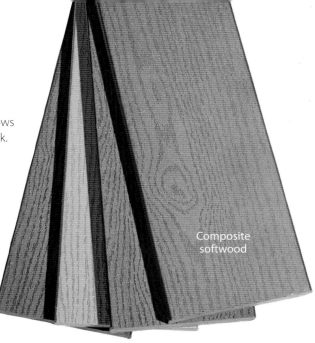

Composite softwood

Brick

LANDSCAPE ARCHITECT
KEN COVERDELL ON

Permeable Concrete

Permeable concrete is created without a sand binder and with a higher rate of cement and recycled fly ash. It's a low-water mix and it has no reinforcing steel in it, so it's faster to form and place but it's more labor because without the additional water it's hard to push around. We call it Rice Krispies because that's what the surface looks like. It's hard to get a uniform color, but it does the job of reducing runoff. Even when compacted with debris, it will allow 3 inches of water to percolate through it per hour, so there's virtually no runoff."

Concrete pavers

Lawns

The curved border of this lawn bleeds into the surrounding shrubs and to a walkway under an arbor of climbing roses that leads to a secluded sitting area.

The traditional American landscape has seemingly always included an expanse of lush, green grass. People took great pride in the condition of their lawns and spent large amounts of time each weekend fertilizing and mowing them.

That was then. Now the watering requirements of a sizable lawn are not only financially out of reach in some areas but downright wasteful where water is scarce. Conserving water has become a key environmental issue, and more and more people are looking for water-wise alternatives to lawns.

It doesn't have to be all or nothing, though. If you love the look and functionality of grass, consider making your lawn a smaller portion of the backyard. Carve out an area for the grass and surround it with hardscaping or native plants

TOP Surrounded by shrubs and lavender, a relatively small area of grass can still feel like a respite in the wild.

BOTTOM Long, thick strands of grass are lovely to lie down in.

LANDSCAPE ARCHITECT
KEN COVERDELL ON

Removing an Existing Lawn

Instead of spraying chemicals on your lawn in order to kill and then remove it, try a technique called sheet mulching. "Put several layers of recycled cardboard over your lawn to cut the light, and then add soil and mulch on top. You can put new, low-maintenance plants into the soil right away, so people don't see the transition that's happening. Over time, the old grass will die without chemicals and the cardboard will decompose into the soil."

that don't require much water. Talk to your local nursery about types of grasses that can survive on very little water, and make sure that the type you select will grow in the amount of shade or sun your backyard gets throughout the day.

Eco-friendly Options

Realizing the need for conservation, growers are stepping up to the plate with solutions. For example, Pennington Seed has come out with Smart Seed, which contains varieties of grass that require less watering and fertilizer and are naturally more drought resistant. The average lawn uses approximately 10,000 gallons of water per year, while Smart Seed requires about 7,000 gallons. It's available at home improvement centers and nurseries across the country.

When you consider that we use potable water to irrigate our backyards, the amount of water a lawn can require seems all the more wasteful. One way to cut back on water usage is to collect rainwater for your lawn. Buy an attractive rain barrel that connects to a hose, or use any form of container that has a lid to keep out mosquitoes.

Xeriscaping is a landscape principle that aims to reduce water use by combining native plants, hardscaping such as patios and walkways, and smaller lawns. The idea is to create a garden that works with nature rather than against it. Along those lines, keeping up a lush lawn in a desert doesn't make as much sense as planting succulents and cactus that have grown and thrived in that environment for centuries. Likewise, a rainy climate can sustain grass, particularly some ornamental varieties, with little intervention.

Another option is synthetic grass, which is not plain old AstroTurf anymore. Companies like SYNLawn offer lines that mimic natural varieties of grass, such as Kentucky blue, fescue, and rye. For a price, you can get the look you want with no mowing or watering, and it stands up to kids and pets too. Some types of artificial grass are even made with recycled materials.

OPPOSITE PAGE Spreading ground covers are a great substitute for grass around this backyard water feature.

TOP A small amount of grass overlooking the swimming pool allows kids to spread out on beach towels on a soft surface.

BOTTOM SYNLawn looks like natural grass, saves water, and stays green in shady areas.

LANDSCAPE DESIGNER
KELLY BOWMAN GREENWOOD ON

Incorporating Artificial Grass

Artificial grass has its place in some garden designs, depending on the situation and what the homeowner wants. "As much as I never thought I'd hear myself say this, there are some good new artificial turf options out there worth considering for problem areas. One of my clients has an oddly shaped flag lot, and the only place for the play area is in a very shady part of the yard. Well-installed artificial grass has the advantage of always looking crisp—even in full shade—and way more lush and attractive than most of the play surfaces out there."

Transition Spaces

Long wooden planks leading to a dining area and a fireplace are softened by lit candles, blooming flowers, and lush grasses.

In addition to planning for patios, decks, and other destination spots in the garden, you'll need to decide how you want to transition from one area to the next. Think about the flow of the space and how to lead foot traffic in a logical direction. Gardens meant for relaxation can get away with gravel paths and people walking over grass to get from one area to the next. But you'll need something more stable underfoot for getting to and from the pool or taking dishes from the outdoor kitchen to the back door of the house.

Paths

The basic purpose of a path may be to lead you from point A to point B, but the journey can be made into a memorable experience, even in a small garden. Plant an eye-catching grouping of flowers at the curve of the path, or place a small fountain there to encourage people to stop and enjoy the scenery before moving along.

Serviceable paths should be at least 2 feet wide, and 3 feet is better for hauling garden equipment or pool supplies. If two people will be walking side by side, a 5-foot-wide path will be most comfortable. Paths can be made of practically any material, from brick, stone, and wood to mulch, gravel, and recycled glass. Stepping-stones are an easy do-it-yourself solution when you just need to walk a few steps over the lawn or ground cover. You can snake them across larger areas, but if it's a path you'll walk on daily, it's better to use a solid material.

Loose materials are cost effective and can also be made to "bleed" into the surrounding plants for less of a manmade look. Be careful, though, not to use loose materials that get stuck in your shoes close to an entrance to the house, or you'll be tracking it inside every time you come in from the garden.

ABOVE A simple wooden bridge connects two sides of the garden that are separated by a natural stream.

RIGHT Lush ornamental grasses billow up around this flagstone path. The twists and turns give the path a more naturalistic look.

BELOW Large stones lead people around a low planter as they make their way across the gravel path to a dining area beyond.

LEFT Large river rocks at the base of the wide wooden stairs pick up on the colors of the slate-tiled patio.

OPPOSITE PAGE, TOP LEFT Bright bougainvillea drapes over a stuccoed wall that leads to this side yard, coaxing visitors beyond the doorway.

OPPOSITE PAGE, TOP RIGHT Ferns and potted flowers line the edge of this side yard and lead the eye toward a curved blue gate. Artfully pruned trees hide the neighbor's house while allowing a view of the richly stained wooden fence.

OPPOSITE PAGE, BOTTOM LEFT Low-maintenance plants that provide color and texture are planted in pots along this narrow side yard. A low stone wall staggers their height and gives the area more dimension.

OPPOSITE PAGE, BOTTOM RIGHT An antique door creates an intimate area for a table and chairs in this narrow side yard.

Stairs

In sloped gardens where stairs are needed, try to make them low and wide so they can also be used as extra seating. If they must be narrow and steep, build a handrail for extra stability and plant around them. Use the same material on the stairs if you have a patio or path made of bricks, straight-edged stone, pavers, or concrete. "Treads should consist of a single stone, not pieces of smaller stones mortared together," says landscape designer William Morrow.

Side Yards

Too often, side yards are used to hide trash cans and recycling or to store bikes and lawn equipment, or they are left to grow weeds. But if the side yard can be used to get from the front of the house to the back, or if any windows in the house look out onto it, include it in your backyard remodel. Visually tie the area into the backyard by using some of the same hardscape materials or plants. If you must store trash there, build a simple structure that matches the style and color of the house to hide containers and keep animals out.

Plant something evergreen in front of windows so you have a pretty view year-round, or choose plants that will attract birds and butterflies for periodic entertainment. If you can hear neighbors or traffic from the side of the house, consider installing an outdoor fountain to mask those sounds. Where houses are built close together, you may lack privacy. In these cases, plant tall shrubs or trees along the fence so you don't always have to keep the shades drawn.

LANDSCAPE CONTRACTOR
BRIAN KOCH ON

Dressing Up Side Yards

When people have a good amount of sun exposure, I like to add espaliered fruit trees in side yards. They hide fencing well and add interest to that area when you look out on it from inside the house."

Trellises

Made from birch twigs, arch-topped trellises combine with flowery clematis to lend character to a featureless wall.

Whether freestanding, bordered by a fence, or covered in vines or flowers, trellises add height and dimension to the garden. They can be made of sleek metal posts and straight-edged wood beams, or something more rustic such as woven willow. Attach a trellis to a wall or fence to give climbing plants something to hang on to, or stick one in a pot to achieve the same end. Fruits and vegetables such as tomatoes and snap peas also need sturdy trellises to climb as they reach toward the sun.

ABOVE This charming Cape Cod–style trellis serves many functions. It frames the view of the house, acts as a simple gate, and offers a place to sit down for a quiet chat.

TOP RIGHT A trellis can be made of anything, even a reclaimed iron bedframe. This one is set between metal garden posts topped with crystal knobs.

BOTTOM RIGHT Match the size and scale of your trellis to what you're growing on it. These delicate spreading trellises are perfect for lightweight climbing vines.

Arbors and Pergolas

A quartet of pergolas surrounds a shaded eating area and supports sweet-smelling jasmine.

TOP This pergola, constructed with concrete columns and thick wooden beams, provides shade for a flagstone patio.

BOTTOM A series of metal arches leads visitors up a grass path studded with wood-beam steps.

Designed to provide relief from the sun's heat, these structures can be spacious enough to cover a large deck, just big enough for one person to pass under, or any size in between. While the terms "arbor" and "pergola" are often used interchangeably, there is a minor distinction between the two structures. Both consist of posts supporting an open roof of beams or lattice, but an arbor is broader and may be connected to a building on one side. A pergola, however, is always freestanding and narrow. Use these features to support climbing plants, tie together different areas of the garden, direct foot traffic, or hide unsightly features.

Landscape designer Katey Mulligan suggests making arbors and pergolas into multipurpose structures. "In addition to providing shade or a focal point in the garden, the structure can be used as a screen to block the neighbor's view or hide a utilitarian area," says Katey.

TOP LEFT Painted white to match the trim of the house, this arbor adds architectural interest to the side yard.

BOTTOM LEFT Surrounded by lavender and rosemary, this metal pergola has a distinct Mediterranean feel.

BOTTOM RIGHT Several arched structures supporting blooming flowers add dimension to the garden and lead people to the gated swimming pool.

OPPOSITE PAGE, TOP This white arbor provides dappled shade over the poolside eating area in a Moroccan-themed backyard.

OPPOSITE PAGE, BOTTOM Well-pruned vines create an almost solid roof on this arbor, which also functions as a passageway to the back door.

LANDSCAPE DESIGNER
KELLY BOWMAN GREENWOOD ON

Adding Style and Value

Adding a pergola or arbor can create architectural interest to subdivision homes that lack character. "Need character and curb appeal? Before my clients add square footage, I always look for opportunities to add style through landscape structures. An attached pergola or arbor is a great opportunity to impose character on a stucco box of a house. Want to take your contemporary place more traditional? Add painted wood trim and detailed woodwork. Wish your stucco box were a Mediterranean dream? Add rustic wood and metal accents. Done thoughtfully, your garden structures can really help your home stand out from the crowd."

Stonescape

Japanese-style lights flank a two-tone deck that stretches across the backyard. A dry streambed studded with ornamental grasses and stones of various sizes runs in the foreground.

OPPOSITE PAGE, LEFT Areas of larger rocks mixed with low plantings create mini destinations. The homeowners believe that each individual stone is important and has its own story, so they chose the larger stones carefully.

OPPOSITE PAGE, RIGHT Glassy black stones set off a sea of predominantly white rock in the meditation area. Adding to the serenity are a granite waterfall and a statue of Buddha amid softly rustling bamboo.

Having lived for several years in Japan, the owners of this San Francisco Bay Area backyard asked landscape designer Patricia St. John to create something that would remind them of that time. They also wanted a dog-friendly design that would require very little water.

To visually connect the backyard to the nearby bay, St. John designed a boardwalk-style deck that leads to various Asian-inspired vignettes. A dry streambed that runs under the deck adds a sense of movement to the garden. Contrasting black and white stones define the meditation area. Because there are so many types of prominent stones in the backyard, St. John used a simple ⅜-inch stone mulch around the ornamental grasses and bamboos. The result is a low-maintenance landscape that feels like home to her clients. "Plus, their active dog has the run of the garden with minimal negative impact," St. John says.

The Elements

- **Decking:** Winchester Grey Trex.

- **Stones:** ⅜-inch Tuscan Gold mulch; Mexican La Paz; ⅜-inch dolomite; 1- to 2-inch cobbles and 3- to 5-inch pamy cobbles in the dry streambed. Individual rocks include Sonoma fieldstone, kryptonite, and basalt.

- **Lighting:** Low-voltage, Asian-style landscape lighting.

- **Water features:** Granite spill fountain and a dry creek.

- **Accessories:** Buddha statue, stone sculptures, and a stone bench.

Harmonious Hardscape

The redwood arbor grounds the house to the landscape and provides dappled shade.

OPPOSITE PAGE, TOP Moss-covered boulders flank an 18-inch-high retaining wall that curves along the edge of the flagstone patio. Low-maintenance shrubs add color and texture.

OPPOSITE PAGE, BOTTOM Raised troughs set in a warm-colored gravel bed contain his-and-hers kitchen gardens.

Landscape designer Katey Mulligan created this serene backyard to serve many purposes. A circular flagstone patio that's large enough for entertaining features a low stone wall with a cap that provides additional seating without the need for space-consuming furniture. The retaining wall also negotiates a minor slope in the backyard and borders a raised planting area. On the other end of the patio, a wisteria-covered redwood arbor flanked by juniper trees frames a decorative concrete pillar.

In a corner of the yard are two large aluminum horse troughs that the homeowners painted a deep bronze color to complement the surrounding golden gravel. The troughs are perfect as raised beds for a collection of lettuces and herbs. Beyond the kitchen-garden area is a small grove of birch trees. Ornamental ducks hide among ferns and the birch trunks.

The Elements

- **Patio:** Dry-laid Connecticut Bluestone "Full Color Range" flagstone.

- **Mulch:** La Paz slate-colored pebbles border the flagstone patio; ⅜-inch Desert Gold gravel in the kitchen garden; wood bark in planting beds.

- **Wall:** 18-inch-high Autumn Creek Wall Rock combined with cool-colored New England Wall Rock; capped with Connecticut Bluestone "Full Color Range" flagstone.

- **Overhead:** Redwood arbor.

- **Landscape:** Plants chosen to tolerate nearby ocean breezes, salty air, and sandy soil; shrubs with vibrant foliage instead of blooming plants and perennials; birch and *Juniperus chinensis* 'Blue Point' trees; kitchen garden.

Chapter 3

Cooking and Entertaining

The backyard is an extension of the house, and that includes the kitchen. When you have a comfortable place to dine outdoors, family meals become special occasions. Similarly, cooking outdoors makes food preparation more fun, especially when all of the tools you need are at hand. In this chapter you'll find information on everything from the best materials for building an outdoor kitchen to creative ways of decorating for outdoor parties. And while we're talking food, we'll give you some ideas on incorporating a kitchen garden, so you can grow, prepare, and enjoy meals in your own backyard.

Outdoor Kitchens

Protected from the sun under a new wooden patio roof, this L-shaped outdoor kitchen is finished with painted stucco to match the house.

Cooking dinner in the backyard can be as simple as grilling steaks on a portable Weber grill and sitting at a picnic table in the middle of the grass. Or it can mean preparing a full meal on a small countertop with a built-in grill and dining in an adjoining seating area with comfortable, well-designed furniture. People who have the space and do a lot of entertaining might even put in a full outdoor kitchen with storage, refrigeration, and a pizza oven.

Designing an Outdoor Kitchen

You don't need much more than a heat source and a long stick to cook outside, but creating something aesthetically pleasing and comfortable to use takes planning. If you like to grill, you've probably experienced trying to balance all of your food and equipment on a small outdoor table and quickly running out of space. Consider building a 6-foot-long counter that has room on either side of a built-in grill to set plates and prepare side dishes. Then, if you start eating outdoors more often, you may want to add a raised counter, hook up a refrigerator, add a small sink, or build an overhead structure for shade.

Most outdoor kitchens are placed near a back door that's close to the indoor kitchen. If you want yours to be farther out in the garden, make sure there's a steady pathway that you can walk across while carrying food and dishes. Also consider the weather where you live. If it's conducive to outdoor dining, then building the kitchen far out into the backyard is a reasonable option. Otherwise, it's better to build something close enough to the back door that you can dash inside to eat if the weather turns.

LANDSCAPE ARCHITECT
KEN COVERDELL ON

Maintenance

Outdoor kitchens will show wear quickly if they aren't properly maintained. "Just because it's stainless steel doesn't mean it won't rust. You need to polish the steel, reseal the countertops, and take care of the mechanical apparatus in ovens and stoves or the outdoor kitchen of your dreams will quickly become too unpleasant to cook in."

TOP This covered outdoor room features a built-in grill, a sleek fireplace, and plenty of seating at both the dining table and built-in bench.

BOTTOM A simple but substantial arbor provides shade for this outdoor kitchen. A built-in grill, fridge, comfy chairs, and stained concrete floors complete the space.

TOP LEFT Stucco can be textured to match the style of your house.

TOP RIGHT Wooden counters have a warm, natural look.

LEFT Brick was the perfect choice for this small counter attached to the side of the house.

BELOW Irregular flagstones create a patchwork pattern on this counter. Two of the doors were salvaged from old furnaces, and the other is made of reclaimed wood.

Counters

If you're starting small, you may choose to build a standard-size counter that's 36 inches high and about 30 inches deep. Be sure you know the size of your grill during the planning stage so that the counter is built to accommodate it. Adding bar seating and a raised counter will encourage family members and guests to sit and talk to the cook, and longer spans of counter-top space will give you plenty of room for helpers who can prepare non-grilled items for the meal.

Outdoor counters are similar in size and functionality to those indoors, but the material choices differ significantly. The substructure is generally made of concrete blocks, though you can also use wood or steel studs covered with cement backerboard. What you cover the substructure with should be coordinated with the style of the house and garden, as well as with the hardscape used elsewhere in the backyard.

CERAMIC TILES can be an economical choice, and they come in a limitless variety of colors, shapes, and surface textures. Before you buy, make sure the tiles will survive in your climate.

STUCCO is applied over concrete block or brick, and it marries an outdoor kitchen counter with a stucco house. While the material is inexpensive, labor can add up, as it will take several days to apply each coat, with time in between for drying. Once it's cured, it needs to be painted right away to protect it from the elements. Hire a skilled professional.

WOODEN CABINETS can be installed in warm, dry climates, but they will age faster than stone, brick, tile, and stucco. Using rustic or reclaimed wood will hide the wear and tear, but whether it's painted or stained, be sure to seal it regularly both inside and out. If you want the look of wood but not the maintenance, consider building the counter out of a composite exterior siding material.

BRICK can be used as the substructure and façade and is often the best choice for an outdoor kitchen built near a brick home. Choose among common brick, reclaimed brick, and brick veneers that are installed like tile but have the same weighty look of full bricks.

NATURAL STONE in the form of flagstone or veneer can be installed over backerboard with mortar and then grouted. Rough-faced stone will give the outdoor kitchen a more rustic look, while square or rectangular stone will have a natural but tidy effect. Faux stone is lighter and easier to install and some types don't require grout, making the façade look like an old garden wall.

This sleek and simple outdoor counter is covered in glazed ceramic tiles. Beyond, mottled tiles in complementary tones surround a simple bench that can be used for seating or for setting food out during parties.

LEFT In desert climates, it's more comfortable to cook and eat in the backyard under a solid overhang with recessed lighting, a ceiling fan, and a fireplace. This outdoor kitchen also boasts stainless-steel doors and a small fridge.

RIGHT Stainless-steel doors and warming drawers complement the built-in refrigerator and grill on this stately brick-and-slate outdoor kitchen. A pair of rotating lights can be pointed toward the grill or the counters.

BOTTOM RIGHT Be sure to buy stainless-steel accessories that will withstand the elements.

Storage and Lighting

To make the counter as efficient as possible, install drawers for small items such as cooking utensils. Also, most countertops are not waterproof, so standing water will eventually seep into the substructure. Be sure to drill holes in the counter's floor so that water can run through, and don't store anything in the counters that can't get wet.

Doors for outdoor kitchens are generally stainless steel, but black powder-coated doors are just as durable and are easier to keep clean. Wooden doors look great but will need to be sealed regularly to prevent warping from water damage. Landscape architect Ken Coverdell advises clients to think about the weather-resistant qualities of every last detail of their outdoor kitchens. "People put in fancy stainless-steel doors, but if they use plated metal

hinges that aren't substantial enough to resist rust, they will fall apart faster than you'd think," Coverdell says.

Don't forget to provide adequate lighting around the outdoor kitchen. Most grills are used for dinner, and you won't be able to see well enough to cook outdoors as the sun goes down without some artificial light. If the barbecue is up against the house, you can wire sconces above it by tapping off existing wires inside the exterior wall. It can be trickier to light outdoor kitchens that are farther out in the backyard. Consider low-voltage lanterns on posts, or string some decorative lights above the grill. You can also get clip-on cordless lights to provide direct light to the cooking surface. "That way you'll be able to tell if your steak is rare or well done," says landscape designer William Morrow.

Countertops

The countertop material you choose for an outdoor kitchen can either let the shape or design of the counter shine or can be the focal point of that area. It should of course be functional and able to withstand the elements, and it can be fabricated with edge details and sink cutouts, just like an indoor countertop. Before you place an order, make sure you know whether the material you picked is suitable for the location you're thinking of, as some materials do best out of the sun or under an overhang.

STONE countertops are an upscale choice and look great outdoors. However, some types of stone aren't suitable because they are too porous or not stain resistant enough. It's best to stay away from softer stones such as limestone and marble, but a granite slab or slate tiles hold up well. All types of stone will need to be treated regularly with an acrylic sealer.

DECORATIVE CONCRETE fits in well with outdoor landscapes and can be colored or textured to your liking. You may choose to have the countertop poured in place or to buy a preformed slab. Countertops made with standard concrete mixes will most likely develop surface cracks over time and can stain easily. There are now mixes that address these problems.

BRICK AND FLAGSTONE don't make smooth working surfaces, but they can be kept relatively clean and fit in nicely when the rest of the unit is made of the same material. Like stone and concrete, they should be resealed regularly.

GLAZED CERAMIC TILES wipe down easily, but the grout will need to be maintained and sealed. Tile is also not as easy to clean because of the irregularity of the surface. But it is a great do-it-yourself option and an inexpensive way to add color to your outdoor kitchen. When selecting a style, be sure it comes with all the accessory pieces you may need, such as bullnose and edge tiles.

COMPOSITES such as quartz or new eco-friendly options that use post-consumer recycled glass in a concrete binder are great choices for outdoor countertops. Choose a design that mimics natural stone, or something wild and crazy that may be too loud indoors but is just right among blooming flowers. Composites should also be resealed to prevent staining.

TOP LEFT Stone tiles are less expensive than slabs but still provide a high-end look.

TOP RIGHT Concrete is a good choice if you want a countertop with some curves. This one features a drain ramp that is perfectly sized to hold the perforated pan, which slides along the molded-in sink lip.

BOTTOM LEFT Natural stone has a rustic, textured surface that looks great outdoors.

BOTTOM RIGHT Use art tiles to spruce up the backsplash on a ceramic tile countertop.

LEFT Concrete counters stained a bright terra-cotta give this outdoor kitchen a European look.

ABOVE Stainless steel was used on everything from the counter and drawers to the grill in this impressive design.

RIGHT TOP Custom concrete countertops bring an artisan quality to the outdoor kitchen.

RIGHT BOTTOM A mitered edge makes this granite slab countertop seem thicker.

Kitchen Materials at a glance

Brick
- **Use for:** Counters and countertops.
- **Pros:** Stately, elegant look.
- **Cons:** The uneven countertop surface must be kept sealed to prevent staining and water penetration.
- **Price:** $–$$
- **Green Tip:** Use reclaimed bricks.

Ceramic Tile
- **Use for:** Counters and countertops.
- **Pros:** Inexpensive, colorful; cap and trim pieces are available for edges.
- **Cons:** Grout needs to be sealed regularly to prevent mold, staining, and water penetration; you must choose tiles rated for your climate.
- **Price:** $–$$
- **Green Tip:** Use tiles that include recycled content.

Composites
- **Use for:** Countertops.
- **Pros:** Composite slabs are easy to keep clean and come in a range of colors and patterns.
- **Cons:** Must be sealed to avoid staining and water penetration.
- **Price:** $$$
- **Green Tip:** Use composite countertops made with recycled materials such as glass in a concrete base rather than pieces of stone in a petrochemical base.

Concrete
- **Use for:** Counters and countertops.
- **Pros:** Blends nicely with concrete patios; withstands the elements; can be tinted, colored, and stamped.
- **Cons:** Most mixes can form surface cracks over time; must be kept sealed to prevent staining and water penetration.
- **Price:** $$–$$$
- **Green Tip:** Ask your contractor to use recycled fly ash in the concrete mix, which helps keep this material out of landfills; use soy-based colorants.

Stainless Steel
- **Use for:** Counters, countertops, and doors.
- **Pros:** Sleek and modern; impenetrable to water.
- **Cons:** High maintenance; must be cleaned and polished regularly; countertop will be easy to scratch.
- **Price:** $$–$$$
- **Green Tip:** Use recycled-steel panels.

RIGHT Landscape contractor Brian Koch combined stone-faced counters with a ceramic tile countertop in a design that will withstand the elements.

BELOW Wooden cabinets must be protected with sealer or paint, both inside and out, to prevent water damage.

Stone

- **Use for:** Counters and countertops.
- **Pros:** Natural material looks good in the landscape; wide range of colors, patterns, and textures.
- **Cons:** Must be kept sealed to prevent staining and water penetration.
- **Price:** $$–$$$
- **Green Tip:** Choose locally quarried stone.

Stucco

- **Use for:** Counters.
- **Pros:** Can help the counter blend in with the walls of a stucco house.
- **Cons:** Surface cracks can form over time.
- **Price:** $–$$
- **Green Tip:** Seal with no-VOC (volatile organic compound) paint.

Wood

- **Use for:** Counters, countertops, and doors.
- **Pros:** Natural material looks good in the landscape; wide range of wood species can be stained many colors; can be sanded and refinished.
- **Cons:** High maintenance; must be kept sealed to prevent stains and water penetration.
- **Price:** $–$$$
- **Green Tip:** Use reclaimed wood or composite wood that includes recycled materials.

Grills and Accessories

A stand-alone grill may be all you need if you cook outdoors only occasionally. Select a model with fold-down side extensions so you'll have somewhere to put the plate of burgers. Building a counter around a stand-alone grill is complicated and not very stable, so if you want a full counter, it's best to buy a built-in grill with a flange that sits on the countertop.

Your next decision will be whether to purchase a gas or charcoal grill. Most people prefer cooking with gas because it's faster and easier—you don't have to wait for the charcoal to heat up. It's also less messy. But there are some cooks who believe that charcoal produces more flavorful food. Though built-in charcoal units aren't as common as gas grills, you can find them. Look for one constructed of powder-coated or porcelain-enameled steel.

For the serious outdoor chef, there are also gas- or propane-powered burners that allow you to prepare non-grilled side dishes. These can be purchased separately or combined with the built-in grill. To complete a full outdoor kitchen, have your builder install a sink, faucet, and refrigerator. "Even if you don't want these amenities at the beginning, it's best to install the drain, water, and electrical lines before you start building, so it's easier and less expensive to add them later," says landscape contractor Brian Koch.

Pizza Ovens

The addition of a pizza oven will make your backyard a popular place for parties. Wood-fired pizza ovens are generally sold as inserts, so you'll need to build a supportive structure around them. The inserts can be made of Italian clay or of refractory concrete combined with firebricks. Both materials will produce pizzas with crunchy crusts. Like charcoal grills, pizza ovens need some prep time. The wood fire will be ready in about 30 minutes, though the pizza needs only a few minutes to cook.

LEFT TOP Large units combining a gas-fired grill and a side burner are great for feeding guests during large parties. This model also has a ledge above the grill for keeping bread warm.

LEFT MIDDLE A cooktop installed away from the barbecue allows a second cook to prepare sauces or pasta while the meat or veggies are being grilled.

LEFT BOTTOM A wood-burning pizza oven can heat up to 750 degrees Fahrenheit with delicious results.

LANDSCAPE DESIGNER
KELLY BOWMAN GREENWOOD ON

Portable Grills

I'm asked a lot to design mobile outdoor kitchens. Whether you're a commitment-phobe or just need a lot of flexibility and don't have a lot of space, wheels don't have to mean lack of style. Pick a spot that commands a view of the whole place—no one likes to have their back to the crowd—and create a 'barbecue garage' or an attractive screen 3 feet high or so. Wheel your grill behind the screen, which itself can be fixed or mobile, and voilà! The impression is of a much more permanent, custom structure suited to the style of the garden. I like to make barbecue garages bar-height so guests can pull up a chair and chat with the chef."

In an outdoor kitchen that has all the bells and whistles, a pizza oven is the cherry on top. Patina on the copper doors gives them an Old World feel.

Dining Outdoors

Of course, you don't need to have an outdoor kitchen to enjoy a meal alfresco. Planning is essential in creating an area that's comfortable to eat in. Sun patterns, wind, privacy, and proximity to the house should all be considered.

While being close to the back door of the house is convenient for hauling food and dishes, sometimes under a shady tree farther out in the yard would be the more comfortable spot for a lingering meal. If the best place for the table and chairs is in an area that gets sun when you'll be outdoors, you can always add a portable umbrella or sun shade, or an overhead structure like an arbor or gazebo (see "Shade Structures" page 150).

Creating a dining area that is somewhat enclosed or protected by low walls or shrubs will help keep table settings in place on windy days. You may want to further protect the area from a neighbor's view by planting trees or placing several containers around the table.

Paving Choices

All of the paving choices discussed in chapter 2 will work for an outdoor dining area, though some are better than others. Decks create a stable and smooth surface to slide chairs around on. Brick, concrete block, and mortared stone are also sturdy options. If you place a table and chairs on irregular flagstone or stone with wide joints that are filled in with plants or gravel, you will have a harder time maneuvering chairs. When that rustic look is desired, try to select lightweight furniture so it is easier to move. For the same reason, landscape designer Katey Mulligan warns against using heavy furniture on crushed gravel. "It can be like trying to move chairs around in quicksand," she says.

LANDSCAPE ARCHITECT CRAIG BERGMANN ON

Plants Under Tables

If you have a stone patio with plants growing in the joints, choose a table with a mesh or glass top so that light and possibly moisture can get to them."

OPPOSITE PAGE An indoor-outdoor room with a solid roof and a heat lamp makes eating in the backyard possible in regions where the weather doesn't always cooperate.

ABOVE This small deck has a gas-powered fire pit that makes eating outdoors feel cozy.

RIGHT A raised, mortared flagstone patio provides a smooth and steady surface for a large outdoor table that seats 12.

BELOW Tall ornamental grasses soften the edges and provide privacy around a simple metal table and chairs.

Outdoor Entertaining

Backyards complete with outdoor kitchens or portable grills and plenty of seating are prime candidates for everything from graduation parties to weddings. When designing a backyard with entertaining in mind, try to create lots of small conversation areas and build low walls that can double as additional places to sit with a small plate and a glass of wine. Walls that are about 14 inches wide and 16 inches high make ideal seating areas. Be sure the wall cap material is smooth enough to sit on comfortably.

When deciding on plants for the backyard, think about the times of year you're likely to entertain and make sure you have plenty in bloom for that season. While you can supplement with candles and strung lights during the party, it's also important to create a lighting plan that softly illuminates the edges of the garden and each gathering area so that guests will barely notice when the sun goes down.

OPPOSITE PAGE Antique metal basins keep beverages cold, while strung tea lights dress up the umbrella. Live plants make perfect centerpieces.

TOP LEFT Outdoor lighting, a white table-cloth, and candles make an evening meal on the patio memorable.

TOP RIGHT This long table, protected from the elements against the house, is used as a buffet during parties. Extra silverware and napkins are housed in the two rolling wooden cabinets underneath.

BOTTOM Providing clusters of seating areas for conversations and dining is ideal in a backyard meant for entertaining.

LANDSCAPE DESIGNER
KELLY BOWMAN GREENWOOD ON

Traffic Flow

Design patios and decks that encourage people to move into the garden. "Alternate functional areas to draw guests into and through your garden. If your living room has doors that lead to the garden, make the area right outside into a dining area. Likewise, a deck or patio adjoining your dining room should be made into a seating area. If two dining spaces are next to each other, what's the point of getting up and moving your iced tea? Great gardens give people a place to go and a reason to go there."

ABOVE Colorful paper lanterns create a festive mood.

BELOW Take a cue from hotels and provide rolled white towels in baskets for guests. When the sun goes down, these candles are ready to be placed throughout the backyard.

OPPOSITE PAGE, TOP LEFT Stainless-steel mini torches add a cheery glow to a pot of succulents.

OPPOSITE PAGE, TOP RIGHT Tin cups holding votive candles lead the way to the party.

OPPOSITE PAGE, BOTTOM Having several seating areas allows smaller groups to mingle and converse.

LANDSCAPE ARCHITECT
CRAIG BERGMANN ON

Torches

I love torches because they say, 'It may be light now, but we want you to stay late into the night.' Make a route with the torches that you want guests to follow if there is something special to see farther out in the garden."

LANDSCAPE DESIGNER WILLIAM MORROW ON

Furniture

"If you run low on seating during a party, pull indoor furniture out to the backyard. It will create a charming, Old World look."

Table Settings

For everyday outdoor meals, consider having a second set of inexpensive plates and glasses so you aren't regularly creating waste with plastic or paper dishware that is meant to be thrown away. One idea is to buy dishes from secondhand stores or garage sales. Collect different patterns, colors, and sizes and mix them together to create a unique table setting.

Special occasions like birthdays and Sunday brunch call for a bit more formality than the average weeknight barbecue. For these events, you may decide to use indoor plates or even fine china, which will instantly create a festive mood. For a centerpiece, select blossoms from the garden, or create a vegetable medley with squash or tomatoes you grew yourself. Fresh herbs floating in a glass bowl of water make a striking and fragrant centerpiece. If you use candles on a windy day, place them inside glass hurricanes to protect the flame.

Deterring Pests

Aside from a sudden burst of rain, the one surefire thing that will ruin an outdoor meal is to be attacked by yellow jackets or mosquitoes. Bees are less aggressive and can generally be kept away if you don't plant flowers they love around the dining area. To deter mosquitoes, make sure there are no containers of standing water in the backyard where they can lay their eggs. Water features that are part of your backyard design should have an aerator to ensure that the water is always moving, making it inhospitable for breeding. If you've done all of these things and still have mosquito problems, you may have to resort to fuel-powered mosquito traps or nontoxic sprays. For people who live in areas where mosquitoes are a problem for months out of the year, screened-in porches are the best option (see page 158).

Yellow jackets love meat and sweet liquids, and they will aggressively go after your food. They tend to nest under roof eaves, in trees, and in the ground, so there isn't anywhere you can set up your outdoor dining area where you're sure to be away from them. Watch for forming nests, though, and buy a nontoxic spray to get rid of the wasps while they're still small. Always spray at dawn or dusk, when there is little activity in the hive. Then wait a couple of days before removing the nest with a stick. To discourage yellow jackets from nesting in your yard at all, be sure to pick up rotting fruit on a regular basis and never leave spilled food lying around.

LANDSCAPE DESIGNER
WILLIAM MORROW ON

Intoxicating Aromas

When entertaining in the backyard, light several incense sticks about an hour before guests arrive. "The fragrance lends an exotic feel to the garden, and it helps keep mosquitoes at bay."

TOP LEFT Centerpieces on outdoor tables need not be elaborate or costly, as these adorable planted terra-cotta pots prove.

BOTTOM LEFT Make placecards into gifts that guests can take home, like these small bottles of olive oil.

OPPOSITE PAGE Dressing an outdoor table with candles, cloth napkins, and ceramic dishes gives it a homey feel. This example looks idyllic under a grand old tree.

Kitchen Gardens

The popularity of organic food and farmers' markets has led to a renewed interest in kitchen gardens. Of course, growing your own food has long been considered a standard part of life in communities around the world. The ease of buying food at the grocery store and living on smaller plots of land made kitchen gardens nearly obsolete, but there is now a growing cadre of enthusiasts who are thrilled to grow their own selection of edibles.

If you're interested in incorporating a kitchen garden into your backyard design for the first time, it's best to start small. Sometimes there's no choice, as there may be little room for growing vegetables and herbs, so look for places that can serve double duty. Landscape designer Patricia St. John suggests building raised vegetable beds that can be used as additional seating: "Build a planter box with the top 18 inches high, and then install pieces of 2 × 6 composite wood on the edges and it becomes a seating area." You can incorporate the raised beds at the edge of a patio. "Plus, by raising the bed, you can put in

LEFT Herbs grow well alongside annuals and perennials in this colorful garden.

ABOVE Building raised beds allows you to grow vegetables in the proper soil rather than having to amend the natural soil in your yard.

RIGHT You don't need a whole bed to grow vegetables. This single white kale grown in a pot thrives in winter.

BELOW Six types of basil provide culinary variety, great color, and a heavenly scent.

rich organic soil, and it will be much easier to plant and harvest the vegetables. Don't make the bed any wider than 3 or 4 feet, so you can reach to the center without having to step into it," St. John says.

When you don't have room for raised beds, or if you want to start even smaller, consider mixing some edibles in with your ornamental plants. Parsley, chard, and lettuces all make great borders. Cooking sages are low growing, while chards and kale have a wonderful variety of leaf colors.

Placement

Before you start thinking about how to incorporate edibles in the backyard, it's advisable to decide what you want to grow. Most vegetables and herbs need a good amount of sun, but look up each variety in *Sunset Western Garden Book* so you'll know that the grouping you want needs the same amount of daily sun. Also, don't build a kitchen garden in an area where storm-water runoff

gathers. Fix any drainage problems you may have before planting.

Some people like to plant herbs and edibles right outside the kitchen door, while others like to use them as an excuse to meander throughout the garden. If you have the space to dedicate a portion of the garden to this purpose, mark off a square or rectangular area and build the traditional four raised

boxes, each containing a selection of compatible edibles. You might grow vegetables in one, herbs in another, and berries in the third, then use the last one for climbing plants such as tomatoes and peas. Again, consult the *Western Garden Book* to make sure you don't overplant each box. With careful planning, you'll be able to have something growing in every season.

OPPOSITE PAGE, LEFT This simple raised bed was built from rot-resistant 2 × 6 redwood.

OPPOSITE PAGE, RIGHT On a patio, use colorful pots to grow herbs and lettuces.

ABOVE LEFT Smack in the middle of the backyard, a Mediterranean herb garden featuring parsley and thyme basks in the sun.

ABOVE RIGHT Rustic branches surrounding these planting beds give them a landscaped look even when fruits and vegetables are not in season.

Well-Equipped Kitchen

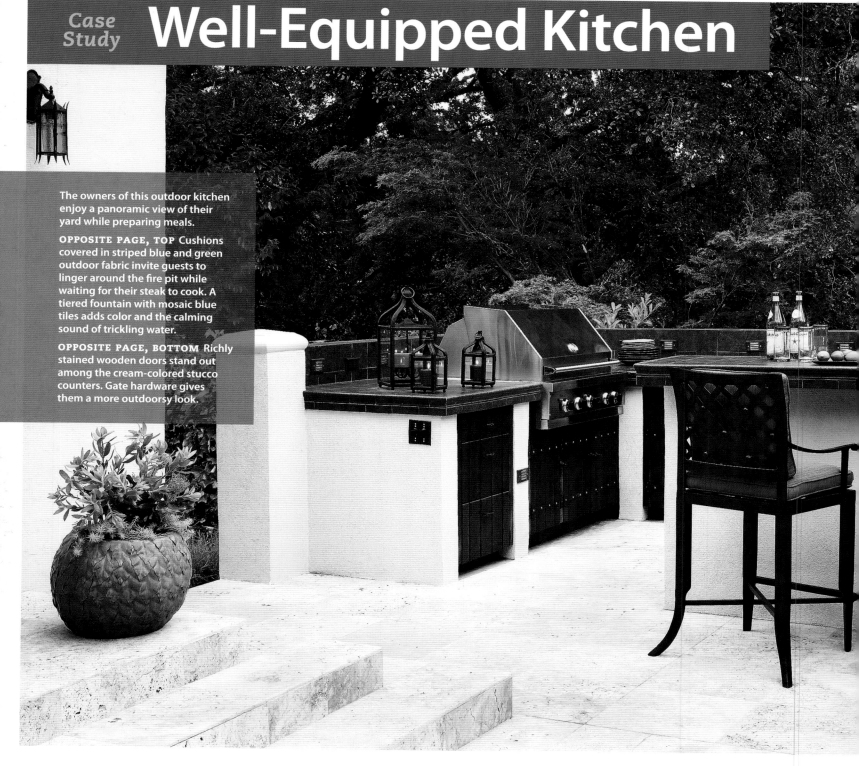

The owners of this outdoor kitchen enjoy a panoramic view of their yard while preparing meals.

OPPOSITE PAGE, TOP Cushions covered in striped blue and green outdoor fabric invite guests to linger around the fire pit while waiting for their steak to cook. A tiered fountain with mosaic blue tiles adds color and the calming sound of trickling water.

OPPOSITE PAGE, BOTTOM Richly stained wooden doors stand out among the cream-colored stucco counters. Gate hardware gives them a more outdoorsy look.

A full outdoor kitchen requires as much planning as an indoor kitchen, as landscape contractor Brian Koch can attest. He built this kitchen next to an existing pool house on an existing concrete pool deck, so meeting the electrical and plumbing needs was a challenge. New electrical service to power the appliances and built-in lighting was brought to the area via conduit laid below the concrete patio, and the sink drain had to be connected to the city sewer line. "A project of this size requires a lot of forward thinking. You've really got to do your homework," Koch says.

The tiled countertops are slightly sloped so that rainwater will drain off. Drainage was also a concern under the counters. Ice machines and refrigerators can leak water when they lose power, and that water needs to be directed away from the area. Because large kitchens like this need to function well, Koch paid attention to standard clearances to make sure multiple cooks

could work together. He also added a pullout trash drawer with separate areas for garbage and recycling, which comes in handy during barbecues. Bar seating on one side allows guests to sit and talk to the cook while others are seated at a nearby dining table. And at the far end of the kitchen is a semicircular seating area ringing a gas fire pit, making this a perfect backyard for entertaining large groups.

The Elements

- **Counters:** Painted stucco.

- **Countertop:** Ceramic tile.

- **Door and drawer faces:** Stained and sealed pine.

- **Hardware:** Cast-iron gate hardware and pulls.

- **Lighting:** Low voltage, integrated into the counter and backsplash.

- **Appliances:** Stainless-steel electric grill, refrigerator, ice maker, and gas burner.

- **Patio:** Jerusalem Gold limestone tile over concrete.

- **Furniture and accessories:** Metal barstools with cushions; low wall for additional seating; throw pillows; market umbrella; gas fire pit; wall fountain.

Garden Geometry

Landscape architect Mark Hershberger designed this kitchen garden at his home in Jackson, Wyoming. Each member of the family has a personal raised bed for his or her own plantings. A metal letter in each bed indicates whose is whose.

Hershberger selected a spot in the garden that gets plenty of sun and is near the outdoor dining area. Each raised bed is constructed with 6 × 6 posts marking the corners and 4-by-4-inch square-grid wire fencing stretched between the posts. The outside framing is 1-by-8-inch cedar boards painted barn red to match the house. Lining the inside of each bed is locally quarried dry-stacked stone that's also used in the driveway, garden walls, and outdoor barbecue. "Everything flows together seamlessly," Hershberger says.

The family plants fruits and vegetables in neat rows and sticks to things that are both delicious and beautiful, such as leaf lettuces, cilantro, parsley, and strawberries. As a result, the kitchen garden always looks great, whether in spring, when plants are just starting to grow, or in summer, when everything is in full production. Even in the dead of winter, when snow covers the beds, the pattern of the raised beds can be admired.

The Elements

- **Hardscaping:** Locally quarried stone set in soil.

- **Landscaping:** Grass.

- **Raised beds:** Posts; wire fencing; cedar boards painted red; stone.

- **Outdoor furniture:** Tabletop made from an old door and painted red.

Chapter 4

Water

Water adds life, movement, and sound to your landscape as no other element can. Swimming pools are magnets for adults and children alike, and they guarantee that your backyard will be filled with people and laughter all summer long. While a swimming pool generates activity, a spa invokes peaceful relaxation. Whether you decide on one or both, this chapter will give you advice on hardscaping and landscaping around them. Also think about adding an outdoor shower to keep people from tracking water through the house after a swim, or incorporating smaller water features such as fountains, garden pools, and waterfalls.

Swimming Pools

For some homeowners, the addition of a swimming pool in the backyard is the fulfillment of a lifelong dream. It's a luxury that can improve the look of your landscape, it's a great draw for parties, and swimming is a heart-healthy form of exercise for people of all ages.

When planning for a new swimming pool, think about how you'll use it most often. Large and deep pools are not necessary for people who just want to splash around with the kids on weekends. Families with small children who want a pool for recreational purposes should consider building one that's only 4 feet deep—enough to splash and swim and play water games but shallow enough to reduce the risk of drowning.

Swimmers should consider long, narrow lap pools. Extending approximately 25 to 40 feet long, these pools allow you to swim a good distance before having to reverse direction, and they needn't be any deeper than 4 feet. For aerobics and games like water polo, the pool needs to be deep enough to allow you to tread water—about 5 or 6 feet.

LEFT Provide plenty of poolside shade so people can spend the entire afternoon lounging by the water.

TOP RIGHT This long and narrow pool looks like a tropical lagoon.

RIGHT Tucked into the corner of the yard, this free-form pool butts right up to the landscape. A spill fountain towers over the deep end.

If entertaining is your motivation, you might take the design up a notch so that the pool goes with the style of the house, add attractive decking, and build storage areas to keep pool supplies and equipment out of sight.

A Long-term Investment

There are many factors to weigh in deciding whether or not to add a pool. Aside from the initial cost, which can range from $6,000 for a simple aboveground pool to $30,000 or more for a large in-ground pool and spa combination, there are also regular operating costs to consider. The average pool holds 20,000 gallons of water. Add a heater and you'll be paying fuel and electricity costs to operate that, plus filtration and purification systems. Ask pool owners in your area what the monthly operational costs are so you aren't caught by surprise. Also call your insurance company to discuss added liability premiums, and consult your city building department to find out whether new fencing will be required for safety. Your property value may also increase, affecting your yearly taxes.

LEFT One of the best ways to keep your pool clean is to keep plants that drop leaves, flowers, and pollen away from it. The landscape around this pool is bright and sculptural, and it's also low maintenance.

BELOW Blooming flowers, topiaries, and climbing ivy create a lush transition between the curves of the pool and the hillside in the distance.

LANDSCAPE DESIGNER
KELLY BOWMAN GREENWOOD ON

Recycling Dirt

When you excavate for a new pool, you end up with yards of dirt that you have to get rid of. "As hauling and dumping fees go through the roof, our landfills max out, and gas prices rise, many homeowners are getting savvy about posting online to places like Craigslist or Freecycle to exchange their dirt. People who are filling in a pool can use the dirt you just excavated. Anytime you can reuse excavated soil on site and avoid hauling it away, you will save money on your landscape project."

Landscaping Around the Pool

Choosing pool decking—the hardscape material immediately surrounding the pool—is an important decision, as it will be the barrier between the water and the rest of the backyard and will catch leaves, grass clippings, and everything else your yard dishes out. The surface must be stable and relatively smooth: not so smooth that you slip when you get out of the pool, but not so coarse that it hurts to walk across with bare feet. Landscape architect Craig Bergmann suggests looking for "a light-colored surface that won't retain heat and burn bare feet. Also be very cautious of rough pool coping that could damage swimming suits when you're getting in and out of the pool." Regardless of the material, make sure the deck slopes away from the pool's coping (the edge of the paving around the pool) by ¼ to ⅜ inch per foot. This slope will allow rainwater to drain away from the pool and prevent pool water that has been splashed out of the pool from flowing back in and bringing dirt along with it.

Removing an Existing Pool

"Half the people who call me want to add swimming pools, and the other half want to fill them in," says landscape designer Kelly Bowman Greenwood. Surprisingly, it can be just as expensive to fill in an existing pool as it is to install a brand-new one. Seriously consider why you want a pool before you commit. "Some of my clients are requesting large in-ground spas rather than full pools so their kids will have a place to splash around but they can still have space for grass. They turn the heat down in summer, and the smaller size really reduces the maintenance burden," Greenwood explains. If you decide to get rid of a pool, the least expensive option is to have your contractor remove the coping and the top of the pool wall, then drill holes in the bottom for drainage. The pool can then be filled and planted over. This part of the yard will never really be the same, though. The best option is to have all of the pool shell broken up and removed. If you ever want to build in this area—a new deck, a pergola, or a home addition—you must compact the dirt. Usually the city or county building department will require a soils engineer to test the compaction and certify that it is stable before you can get a permit to build.

Alternatively, take advantage of the large hole in your yard by putting in an underground cistern that collects rainwater to be used for irrigating the landscape. This is a great way to conserve water, but check with your local building department first to see if it's allowed in your area.

Stained and scored concrete creates a smooth, cool walking surface around the pool.

LEFT Brick decking has an elegant and traditional look, requires little maintenance, and can be laid in a variety of patterns.

ABOVE Composite decking is a better choice than natural wood around swimming pools because it stands up to water and doesn't splinter.

RIGHT Stone tiles cut in three sizes are mortared in place, creating a smooth and stable surface for heavy lounge chairs.

Pool Decking at a glance

Brick

- **Pros:** Easy to maintain, durable.
- **Cons:** You need to keep moss from growing on brick, as it makes the surface slippery.
- **Price:** $–$$
- **Installation:** On sand or mortared onto a concrete slab; choose SX-rated bricks if you live where the ground freezes and thaws.
- **Green Tip:** For a bit more money, you can buy salvaged bricks.

Composite Decking

- **Pros:** Durable, won't splinter, provides excellent traction for wet feet, resists rotting and insects, and doesn't need to be resealed.

- **Price:** $$$
- **Installation:** Similar to that of wood decking; some brands use proprietary fastening systems.
- **Green Tip:** Composites are an eco-friendly choice because they are made from sawdust and recycled plastics.

Concrete

- **Pros:** Wide variety of colors and designs; easy to maintain.
- **Cons:** Can be slippery when wet, so give it a brushed or textured finish.
- **Price:** $$–$$$
- **Installation:** Should be done by a professional with plenty of experience.

- **Green Tip:** Ask your contractor to use recycled fly ash in the mix and to use nontoxic pigments if you're adding color.

Concrete Pavers

- **Pros:** Widely available in many shapes and colors; easy to replace damaged pavers.
- **Price:** $–$$
- **Installation:** Requires a permanent border to prevent shifting; pavers are installed over compacted gravel topped with bedding sand.
- **Green Tip:** Permeable pavers allow rainwater to seep into the ground rather than run off into local storm drains, polluting water supplies.

Paving Stones

- **Pros:** Textured surfaces make them slip resistant around a pool; can have a formal or informal look depending on how the pieces are cut.
- **Cons:** Irregularities and height differences can become tripping hazards.
- **Price:** $$–$$$
- **Installation:** Can be laid over a sand base or mortared onto a concrete slab.
- **Green Tip:** Choose paving stones that are quarried locally.

Wood

- **Pros:** A variety of wood species allows for many design options; a natural look.
- **Cons:** Wood requires seasonal maintenance, such as sanding and sealing, which is especially important around the pool.
- **Price:** $–$$$
- **Installation:** Most often seen surrounding a pool installed in a raised deck.
- **Green Tip:** Choose sustainably harvested species and finish with low-VOC stains and sealants.

ABOVE Concrete pavers pick up the colors of the natural stone walls and are more affordable than stone tiles placed across the entire pool deck.

Spas

Portable spas can be set anywhere in the backyard. This one has a commanding view of the patio and lawn.

TOP Low ornamental grasses planted in a trough around the spa, along with potted bamboo, provide a bit of privacy.

MIDDLE Jetted spas soothe aching muscles. Water from this spa pours out into the pool, creating pleasing sounds and helping to heat it.

BOTTOM Though separated from the pool, this spa feels like a well-designed part of the overall landscape because it uses the same stone edging as the nearby raised planter, and the same blue tiles as the main pool.

Soaking in a spa or hot tub is a great way to relax after a stressful day. The spa's hot water warms your muscles, creating a similar sensation to having a massage. However, hot water isn't safe for everyone—check with your doctor first if you have heart disease or blood-pressure disorders. Pregnant women should also consult with their physicians before spending time in a spa.

An in-ground spa is almost always connected to a swimming pool and shares its water filtration and heating equipment. If you don't have a pool or don't want to take on a large landscaping project by adding an in-ground spa to an existing pool, consider a portable version. You can build a low deck around the spa to give it the look of a built-in. Most models are easy to set up and include all the necessary pipes, filters, and heaters.

Location

If you have the option of choosing the location for your spa, place it in a sheltered and out-of-the-way area for privacy. Otherwise, you can add potted plants, fencing, or an arbor to create these conditions. Portable spas must be set on a solid surface—a concrete slab is ideal. Setting it directly on soil won't work, as the weight will cause the spa to settle unevenly over time. Before putting a portable spa on an existing deck, make sure the structure is in good enough condition to handle the weight.

Outdoor Showers

A maroon stucco wall provides a private place to shower and hides the plumbing. The large cutout makes it feel less like an obstruction, and the ledge is a great place to set towels.

One way to keep your pool or spa clean is to have people rinse off before taking a dip. Having an outdoor shower makes this more convenient, especially for guests. It's also handy for rinsing any chemicals off your skin and hair after a swim.

Location

The least expensive way to construct an outdoor shower is to tap into an existing water source. Tapping into a spigot used for irrigation will work, but you'll have only cold water to shower with. Instead, try to locate the shower near the point where hot- and cold-water pipes enter your home. Or you can build the outdoor shower on an exterior wall opposite an interior bathroom or kitchen that has hot- and cold-water pipes running through the wall.

Your landscape contractor can install a drainpipe that connects to your home's main sewer line so that shower water doesn't flood the area or run toward the house. Another option is to build a dry well, allowing shower water to slowly absorb into the surrounding soil. This option works only if you won't be using soap or shampoo in the shower (see tip box below).

If you might use the shower for more than just a quick rinse, build it in a private area where bathing suits are optional. Add a shower door or curtain, or plant some tall shrubs around the area.

Materials

Design your outdoor shower with the style of your home and landscape in mind. If the shower is up against the house, you don't have to add tile to the wall, as the house siding material should be weather resistant enough to handle the job. The shower floor can be a concrete slab with tile on top, wood decking with gaps in between the boards to allow water to drain through, or dirt with a few flagstone pavers filled in with ground cover.

LANDSCAPE ARCHITECT CRAIG BERGMANN ON

Shower Runoff

Before building an outdoor shower, give some thought to whether you will use it for showering or just rinsing. "If you want to use shampoo and soap, you really must connect drainage to your sewer or septic system. Otherwise, the residual runoff could cause great damage to surrounding plants."

TOP This large stone shower features a corner sink, a rain-style showerhead, and a drain leading to the main sewer system.

ABOVE LEFT Installing the shower fixture on the side of the house allows you to tap into existing plumbing lines. If your siding is in good condition, it can handle the extra splashes.

ABOVE RIGHT A repurposed tub and shower faucet attached to a tree trunk makes a simple outdoor shower. The water runoff seeps between the wide joints of the flagstone courtyard.

Water Features

A water bowl of Mexican canterra stone burbles in a casual, gravel-lined courtyard. The 42-inch-diameter bowl sits on an industrial-strength grate atop a wide concrete basin. Water flows over the edge, filters through the gravel, and is recirculated back into the bowl.

There's nothing like water to reinforce a connection with nature and stimulate the senses. Large garden pools or those that incorporate waterfalls can make spectacular focal points in the backyard, but sometimes it's best to start small.

As long as it's sealed properly, nearly any container can be turned into a backyard water feature. Look for wide and shallow pots, terra-cotta planters, or reclaimed materials such as wine barrels and claw-foot bathtubs to turn into small garden pools.

Location

Walk through the garden and think about where the best place for an aboveground or in-ground water feature would be. Mark out possible areas and shapes with a garden hose and lay a mirror on the ground to see what the water will reflect. Position the water feature where its reflection will showcase nearby trees or rolling hillsides, or simply the full moon at night.

As with swimming pools, you'll want to keep garden pools away from certain types of trees and plants that will load it with debris. The cleaner the water, the less maintenance you'll have to do. If you plan to grow plants in a pond, position it where the plant species you want will get the right amount of light. In hot climates, avoid placing a garden pool in direct sunlight, as the water may heat up and evaporate quickly.

Naturalistic Pools

A well-designed garden pool can blend seamlessly into the landscape, especially when plants grow right up to and even in the water. The key is to eliminate square corners and hide manmade edges. This is a great solution in tight spaces because the pool can meander from one area to the next as space allows, rather than having to fit in a square or rectangular space.

ABOVE A lot of planning is required to create a garden pool that looks like it sprang up from nature, but a result like this makes it well worth the effort.

RIGHT A square concrete garden pool is dressed up with the color and texture of succulents. The homeowners can enjoy the sound of the gurgling fountain while dining outdoors.

BELOW Moving water attracts birds. The urn in the middle of the aboveground pool is filled with stones, and it leaves a half-inch ledge for birds to bathe and drink in.

LANDSCAPE DESIGNER
WILLIAM MORROW ON

Water Feature Styles

Naturalistic water features with stone waterfalls are very difficult to execute well. They require large amounts of stone being imported to the site to avoid a theme-park look. If on a budget, go with a purposeful, manmade look, like a cistern, trough, or vessel. A simple rectangular koi pond is my favorite."

Fountains and Waterfalls

Moving water, whether it's a small trickle from a wall fountain, a gurgling spray fountain, or a high waterfall, adds life to the backyard and blocks street noise. Again, using almost any container with the addition of a simple pump bought at a home improvement center, you can create all kinds of moving-water features.

Fountains that look as though the water spills into the ground are actually sitting on top of catch basins that recirculate the water back into the water feature. These can make great weekend projects. For information on how to build your own, consult Sunset's *Garden Pools, Fountains, and Waterfalls.*

Wall fountains seem more complicated, but the same principles apply: Water gets sucked into a pipe from a basin that can be above or below ground and then falls back into the basin. The water may come out of a mask hung on the wall, a ledge that creates a wide sheet of water, or a simple pipe. The more water that drops, the louder the sound.

True waterfalls are created at transition points in streams. You can re-create such natural occurrences in your backyard by artistically arranging stones and boulders to allow for several spots where water can fall from one area to the next. It's best to have a natural slope in your garden, but you can also use the soil excavated for the water feature to add height. The placement of the stones determines the character and sound of your waterfall and is truly an art. Hire a landscape designer or contractor who has built realistic-looking waterfalls in the past.

OPPOSITE PAGE, LEFT The warm terra-cotta color of the concrete wall, draping bougainvillea, water lilies, and fish make this simple wall fountain look as though it's in an Old World courtyard.

OPPOSITE PAGE, RIGHT A sloped lot with lush vegetation makes it easier to create a realistic-looking waterfall.

ABOVE LEFT Water rushes down the face of this stone retaining wall with enough force to create bubbles at the bottom. Pick your materials based on what they look like when wet.

ABOVE RIGHT Waterfalls are popular features in desert landscapes. This waterfall is fed from the pool below.

LANDSCAPE DESIGNER
PATRICIA ST. JOHN ON

Waterfall Safety

Families with small children are often concerned about the safety of large water features. "I once designed a pondless waterfall where, at the end of its journey, the water went into a stone-and-gravel bed and recirculated back to the top through underground tubes. The family still got the sound of moving water but without the risk."

In a backyard dedicated to plants, a wall fountain is the element that grounds the design.

OPPOSITE PAGE, LEFT Water shoots out of a simple metal spigot into a dark lagoon below that's filled with water plants and floating lily pads.

OPPOSITE PAGE, RIGHT Blooming rosebushes cascade down an ivy-covered wall, perfuming the seating area.

Landscape designer William Morrow uses his long and narrow terraced lot primarily as a testing ground for plants. "I needed a flexible space where I could experiment with new cultivars and varieties to see how they perform in the Washington DC area," he says. "I continually pull up plants that underperform and install the latest rare plant that I'm able to procure."

The sensible pea gravel path, low stone walls, and barberry hedge give the backyard symmetry and order, preventing it from looking like an out-of-control test garden. But the focal point is a simple fountain in the middle terrace, surrounded by a curved wall and filled with water plants. The sound of water creates a peaceful calm in the garden. A pair of agaves sit in pots on stone columns that flank the wide stairs leading from the seating area to the garden beyond.

The Elements

- **Water feature:** Wall fountain.

- **Hardscaping:** Pea gravel path; retaining walls made of Carderock Stone quarried in Maryland; stone and concrete stairs.

- **Furniture and accessories:** Metal seating; slate-topped table; potted plants throughout the garden.

Chapter 5

Kids and Pets

When remodeling a backyard, consider the needs of every member of the family. Kids love to be outdoors, so make the backyard a place where they can play safely for hours on end. Some families will decide to incorporate a play structure such as a tree house, or equipment that encourages sporting activities. Other families may forgo play equipment and create a garden that inspires imagination with kid-friendly plants and structures that can be turned into a pirate ship one day and a castle the next. Pets are important members of the family as well. Make the backyard a safe place for them to be in unattended, and choose hardscaping and plants that are tough enough to withstand any abuse.

LOVE LAUGH

Inside this 8-by-12-foot cabin are a mini-kitchen, a small table-and-chairs set, and a cozy loft space.

Landscape designers are often asked to make a backyard fun and friendly for kids. Depending on the family, the task may be to create a safe area for children to play and imagine, or it may be to incorporate a climbing structure or playhouse that doesn't dominate the space. In designing your kid-friendly garden, remember that every area should encourage multiple activities. Also make sure the backyard will be able to grow and change as your kids do.

Playhouses

Children love to pretend that they are adults. Playhouses are so appealing because they give kids a place of their own that looks and feels like the real thing. If you're handy with tools, consider building your own playhouse using recycled materials. Search for local salvage yards that can supply you with old windows and doors and even hardwood flooring and fixtures.

When you don't have the time or the tools to do it yourself, there are other options. Storage sheds sold at home centers can easily be retrofitted into playhouses with decorative items such as house numbers and a doorbell, and you can even paint one to look like a house. Many companies sell playhouse kits that can be shipped to your home. Styles are standardized, but they can incorporate design elements such as real roof shingles and wraparound porches. Custom-built playhouses are the most expensive option. Some include finishing touches such as crown molding and electric lights.

ABOVE This cabin-style playhouse kit arrived with preassembled walls. It looks quaint tucked into a corner of the garden.

RIGHT Sheets of plywood and a market umbrella were transformed into a fairy princess castle with the help of purple paint, gate hardware, and ribbons. Two potted plants add to the cheery effect.

BELOW In a woodsy setting, this large play structure with a green roof and slide almost blends in with its surroundings.

LANDSCAPE DESIGNER
KELLY BOWMAN GREENWOOD ON

The Right Structure

Do you really want a giant wooden play structure in the middle of the yard, or something smaller like a tire swing tucked away in the corner? Include your kids in the decision. Also pay attention to what they use most in the park to get an idea of what they will respond to. If you have several kids, have at least one area that each age group will be interested in. Try not to have them overlap, so that older kids are less likely to bowl over younger ones."

LEFT A 14-by-14-foot sandbox has plenty of room for multiple kids and their toys.

BOTTOM LEFT It won't be as fun for school-aged children, but toddlers will enjoy a small sandbox like this one tucked into the corner of a yard.

BOTTOM RIGHT Flat areas can be used for making mud pies or simply smushing sand around. Check underneath regularly for spiders, though, as they love dark spaces.

BUILD THE SANDBOX with some type of border to contain the sand. But leave the bottom of the box unenclosed so water can drain out. Think about adding a flat ledge for kids to work on, either as the border or as a separate piece inside the box.

THE BEST SAND for playing in contains clean, round grains of the same size so that it doesn't get too compacted when wet. You'll need more than you might think—32 cubic yards for a standard 4-by-8-foot box that's 12 inches deep. All-purpose sand doesn't have uniform grains. "Play sand" does, but it and all-purpose sand can contain fine shards of crystalline silica, which has been linked to lung disease in people who are exposed to it daily. Look for sand that specifically says it doesn't include crystalline silica.

KEEP ANIMALS OUT of the sandbox by covering it when it's not in use. If your sandbox doesn't have a fitted hard cover, you can install a mesh or tarp cover to fit. Hold the mesh in place with metal hooks screwed to the outside of the sandbox.

Sandboxes

Among the least obtrusive defined play areas for kids are sandboxes. Their color and shape can be made to blend into the rest of the garden, plus water and sand are natural materials that can be used together for hours of fun.

There are a few general guidelines regarding placement of a sandbox. Reduce the amount of sand that gets tracked onto your patio or into the house by locating the sandbox a good distance from those areas. A gravel path or lawn creates a good transition. Also consider the sun exposure of the proposed site. While you want to keep children out of direct sunlight, some is needed to keep the sand dry and sanitary. The best option is an area that gets some sun during the day. Finally, make sure that a water source is nearby so that a hose can reach over to the sandbox for building castles.

This sandbox looks like a natural part of the landscape. Water pipes were brought to the area, and the spigot is equipped with a self-closing shower valve so the kids can't accidentally leave the water running.

Climbing Structures

Swings, slides, and things that can be climbed on and jumped off of are popular with most children. The best climbing structures offer elements that can be used for more than one purpose and that can be changed and updated as kids get older. Because these large structures take up a lot of space, especially when you take into account the surrounding safety zones, they aren't feasible in small backyards. If this is the case, incorporate vertical structures like climbing walls, or plan for garden walls that can also be used as balance beams.

SAFETY ZONES are an important element around climbing structures. There should be soft surfacing clear of obstructions extending 6 feet out from all equipment that children could fall off. At the bottom of a slide, the safety zone should equal the height of the slide (in linear feet from top to bottom) plus 4 feet.

CHOOSING THE RIGHT STRUCTURE for you depends on many factors. If your kids already have access to a large climbing structure at a local park or at school, they may not be as interested in one at home, where there are most likely fewer kids to play with. But if you have a large backyard and live where there isn't ready access to another climbing structure, it might make sense to incorporate one. Home centers sell plans that include shopping lists for the right amount of raw lumber and fasteners, or you can buy kits of precut pieces already drilled for bolts and stained. You can put the kits together yourself or hire a professional. Custom-designed play structures will give you exactly what you want, but they are the most expensive option.

INCREASE THE PLAY VALUE of the set by adding extras that encourage kids to use their imaginations. Peepholes, bells, fun-house mirrors, steering wheels, and rope ladders will extend the life of the play structure by letting it be a pirate ship one day and a haunted mansion the next.

OPPOSITE PAGE, TOP LEFT A hanging climber like this would also work on its own in most small spaces.

OPPOSITE PAGE, TOP RIGHT Accessories like this one don't cost much and can add an enormous amount of play value to climbing structures.

OPPOSITE PAGE, BOTTOM Kids can stay active for hours on this structure, so the parents wisely included a swinging bench and Adirondack chairs where they can observe the action.

ABOVE Custom structures allow your kids to choose their own theme and colors, but they come with a hefty price tag.

Tree Houses

There's something magical about having your own place up in the trees. Choosing the best tree and getting the foundation right are the trickiest parts. After that, the construction is similar to that of a playhouse. Consult an arborist to make sure the tree or trees you want to use are healthy and strong. Then you can design the tree house to incorporate features such as drawbridges, ladders, and lookouts.

Landscape architect Ken Coverdell suggests using recycled materials like old house parts to make playhouses and tree houses look more realistic. "Go to a local salvage yard and select old doors and windows to give your play structure some architectural character. It's also a great way to save money on extras such as doorknobs, hinges, and even lumber."

Swings

Kids of all ages enjoy swings, and once you have the support structure built, you can change out the swings as your children grow. Babies and toddlers should use full-bucket swings that protect them from leaning too far forward or backward. Half-bucket seats that have a chain across the front are safe for preschoolers, while kindergarten-aged children can start using standard swings or tire swings. When older children get bored with traditional swings, they can try disk seats, bouncy swings, and trapeze swings.

Landscape architect Craig Bergmann says to "look for a great tree branch in the backyard to hang a swing from. This will be much smaller than manufactured swing sets and just as fun. Then incorporate plants and paths to make getting to the play area a journey in itself and kids will love it."

LEFT Instead of having a ladder, this tree house features a drawbridge that leads to the family deck.

RIGHT A cabin-style tree house with a corrugated metal roof looks idyllic in this cluster of tree trunks.

MIDDLE These two swings are hung from a beam covered with a climbing vine that hides the structure, helping it blend into the surrounding landscape.

BOTTOM Sometimes a grand old tree and a simple tire swing are all you need.

Ramps

For kids who enjoy testing their physical limits on skateboards or BMX bikes, a ramp takes the sport to a whole new level. The materials are inexpensive, but the structures themselves can be an eyesore. Use exterior-grade plywood to build a skate ramp, and it will be light enough to move out of the way when you need the space. Ramps or quarter-pipes can be placed on a smooth skating surface, but half-pipes should be surrounded by wood chips or another soft landing material.

Trampolines

Exhilarating, challenging, and, yes, a little dangerous, trampolines are often found in the backyards of people who have skateboarders and gymnasts in the family, because they're great for practicing tricks.

If your kids want a trampoline but you're worried about the risk factor, there are a few things you can do. Consider building the trampoline over a hole in the ground and installing the mat at ground level so that there won't be any falls from an elevated surface. Newer trampolines are sometimes offered with netting to prevent jumpers from falling off the sides. Also consider spring-free trampolines, so kids won't hurt themselves if they land on the edge of the bouncing surface. Whatever kind you go with, make sure that the trampoline is surrounded by a soft landing surface and that it's away from other structures, trees, and power lines.

TOP LEFT This roller coaster for bikes was made out of scrap wood and provides the perfect level of challenge for smaller kids.

TOP MIDDLE Use assorted firewood, dirt filler, and a piece of plywood to make a ramp for bikes to jump off of.

TOP RIGHT The challenge in constructing a skate ramp is getting the curve just right for liftoff.

BOTTOM LEFT Side safety nets make the decision to get a trampoline easier on parents.

BOTTOM MIDDLE Snowboarders, divers, skateboarders, and gymnasts can all use trampolines to practice their skills.

BOTTOM RIGHT An in-ground trampoline is not only safer, but also it visually recedes into the landscape.

TOP LEFT These boys use the court to play basketball with Dad and race around on scooters. Choose a hoop that can be adjusted in height as the kids grow.

TOP RIGHT Guests can sit and eat at this large table while waiting to take turns playing bocce.

BOTTOM LEFT These homeowners used copper figures that look like garden art instead of traditional chess pieces.

BOTTOM RIGHT If you have the space for a sizable putting green like this one, playing golf in the backyard can become a group activity.

Sports Courts

Keep your front driveway from being cluttered with sports equipment by pouring a concrete patio in the backyard that can serve multiple purposes. Put a basketball hoop at one end and it becomes a half-court for one-on-one games. Two posts and a net can turn it into a volleyball or badminton court. The concrete surface can also be used for riding bikes or scooters and drawing chalk murals.

Bocce Courts

An ancient game that's fun for people of all ages, bocce is similar to bowling. All you need are a flat, level surface of gravel and a set of bocce balls. Regulation courts are 76 feet long and 10 feet wide, but you don't need an area that large to play.

Chess

It's easy to turn any square area of lawn or low-lying ground cover into a chessboard. Choose two colors of square pavers (32 of each color), set them apart evenly as you would stepping-stones, remembering to alternate colors, and you have a life-size game board. When the pieces are removed, you can enjoy the area as a patio.

Putting Greens

Avid golfers can practice putting and chipping in the backyard with even a small putting-green area. You can install a real bent-grass green or a synthetic green that doesn't need to be mowed and watered and will always be at the perfect putting length.

LEFT Wood mulch is a good choice under climbing walls.

ABOVE Grass looks beautiful, but it will take a beating under a play structure and it won't provide the needed cushioning for big falls.

RIGHT Rubber mulch comes in an array of playful colors, from brown to purple, and provides a softer landing for kids falling off swings, slides, and monkey bars.

Play Area Surfaces at a glance

Grass

- **Pros:** Aesthetically pleasing; feels good on bare feet.
- **Cons:** Doesn't provide enough padding under areas where children might fall from a couple of feet off the ground.
- **Price:** $–$$
- **Maintenance:** Uses a large amount of water and requires regular mowing.
- **Green Tip:** Use synthetic grass to eliminate water needs.

Sand and Pea Gravel

- **Pros:** Provides good cushioning at depths of 9 inches or more.
- **Cons:** Compacts in rain; easily tracked through the garden; hard to walk on.
- **Price:** $–$$
- **Maintenance:** Requires continuous leveling, sifting, and periodic breakup of compacted sand and gravel.
- **Green Tip:** Look for silica-free sand.

Wood Chips and Wood Mulch

- **Pros:** Provides good cushioning at depths of 9 inches or more.
- **Cons:** Compacts with use and exposure; decomposes over time; susceptible to microbial growth.
- **Price:** $
- **Maintenance:** Requires periodic replacement and continuous leveling and sifting to remove dirt.
- **Green Tip:** Use wood chips from recycled sources.

Rubber Mulch and Rubber Tiles

- **Pros:** Mulch provides superior cushioning at the appropriate depth and does not deteriorate or become compacted; rubber mulch lasts longer than natural mulch; tiles won't get tracked through the garden or appeal to pets.
- **Cons:** Tiles have an industrial look; some colors of rubber mulch lack a natural appearance.
- **Price:** $–$$
- **Maintenance:** Mulch requires some leveling and sifting; tiles can be hosed down.
- **Green Tip:** Use a recycled product.

Wooden beams border the gravel under this play structure, which helps keep the material from migrating into the grass.

Family Gardens

W hat if you don't want to incorporate a playhouse or a climbing structure—either because you don't have the space or don't like the look? There are still plenty of ways to create a garden that's kid friendly. All you have to do is think like a kid. Get down on their level and look around the garden. Are there any plants that are fun to touch? Paths that lead to secretive places? Water features that pose no safety risks but are reachable by small children? Designing an accessible garden without dictating a particular activity allows kids the most creative freedom.

Pure Imagination

"A friend of mine once told me that when she was young the most important feature in her backyard was a large tree root," says landscape designer Patricia St. John. "She had more fun in that area of the garden where her imagination could run wild than any play structure could have given her."

Kids love areas where they can hide. If you have a place in the garden hidden by shrubs or trees, you'll find that kids will turn that area into a fort without your having to build one. Hardscaping can entertain children as well. A continuous path through the garden is fun for them to bike or rollerblade on. Try to create several areas that appeal to children, rather than just one, so kids can move throughout the garden and create their own adventures every day.

LANDSCAPE ARCHITECT
CRAIG BERGMANN ON

Paths for Kids

K ids love to run or ride their bikes on paths. "Create a network of kid paths that are narrow. Maybe even design them with height restrictions so that adults can't follow—say, under low-branching trees or shrubs. The more mysterious without being dark or creepy, the better."

OPPOSITE PAGE Using bits of jewelry, toys, and improvised art pieces, parents and kids worked together to decorate the mortar that holds stone steps in place.

TOP This secluded side yard offers plenty of places to play hide-and-seek, along with plants to dart in and out of.

BOTTOM Even in a small courtyard garden, have at least one area that functions at a child's level.

Plants

Make sure you don't have any poisonous plants in your yard, and remove anything prickly from areas where you want kids to be able to play. If a plant has berries, they should be edible. The best plants for kids are those that have play value. "Plants that produce pods or are ticklish or soft are popular with small children," says landscape designer Kelly Bowman Greenwood.

Plants that attract wildlife may also be a bonus in a kid-friendly garden. Butterflies and hummingbirds are fun to chase, but minimize plants that attract bees.

Water Features

Wall fountains and spill fountains give your backyard a relaxing feel and block noise from neighbors, and they can also be fun for kids. As long as there is no standing water that children could fall into, there won't be any drowning risk. Wall fountains can be set up to pour into a gravel-covered container underground where the water is then recirculated.

Try taking a pot that's a few feet high and has a narrow neck and turning it into a spill fountain. Kids will love to see and touch the shiny water as it cascades down the sides. The pot should be tall and narrow enough that curious kids can't fall in.

OPPOSITE PAGE, TOP LEFT Planted to look like a garden that fairies would live in, this backyard features fuzzy lamb's ears, lady's-mantle that catches water droplets from dew or rain, and holiday lights threaded into the trellis.

OPPOSITE PAGE, TOP RIGHT Made by an artist partly out of recycled oxygen tanks, this water feature doubles as garden art and a place to play. The kids collect dribbles of water to use in the sandbox and make music by banging on the bells.

OPPOSITE PAGE, BOTTOM This bubbling fountain has only an inch of water on its surface. It's low enough for kids to splash in, without posing much of a safety risk.

RIGHT Surrounded by potted plants, this simple wall fountain is entertaining for children and looks great in the garden.

LANDSCAPE DESIGNER
KATEY MULLIGAN ON

Plants for Education

Growing herbs and vegetables is a great way to show kids where food comes from. Include children in everything from planting the seeds to harvesting to give them a sense of accomplishment and pride in what they are eating."

Petscaping

A winding path made of wood planks gives dogs a place to run. On either side, smooth flagstones set in pebbles and small cedar chips are comfortable on paws.

W hile kids can certainly affect the design and function of your backyard, animals present their own set of challenges. If you have pets that are allowed out-doors, especially ones that spend time unattended in the backyard, make sure the landscape is nontoxic and durable.

Dogs

Just like when you childproof inside the house, if you have a dog you need to think about what could possibly harm him in the yard. Keep garden supplies and chemicals locked up in the garage or shed. "Think breed-specific. Golden retrievers will eat anything, while some other dogs will dig under things or jump over them," says landscape designer Kelly Bowman Greenwood.

The key is not to fight against the inevitable. "If you want a lawn, make it a geometric shape so that it's easier to re-sod after the dog tears it up," Greenwood explains. Landscape architect Craig Bergmann suggests that dog owners shy away from tender plants that could be ruined if a dog lies on them repeatedly, and plants that attract a lot of insects.

Chickens

Not every family has chickens (nor are they allowed in residential areas in many cities), but those who do find they are lots of fun for kids. Chickens are amusing to watch as they peck around the garden, chasing them often results in a little airborne lift, and baby chicks will bring out the parenting instinct in your little ones. Gathering eggs to make Sunday breakfast will also provide a lesson in where food comes from.

TOP LEFT If your dog will be outdoors for most of the day or at night, give him a place to sleep and stay out of the sun.

TOP RIGHT This dog-friendly backyard has sturdy wooden furniture, a high fence, and a gravel patio.

BOTTOM Chickens make great pets, plus collecting eggs is a great job to give small children in the garden.

LANDSCAPE DESIGNER
WILLIAM MORROW ON

Hardscaping for Dogs

P ea gravel or decomposed granite is one of my personal favorites. It's a sophisticated, European look, and I recommend it to anyone with dogs. It makes it much easier to clean up after them, and, surprisingly, they will prefer it over grass or other areas in the garden."

Playing House

It's the details that make the difference. Pink shutters, window boxes, gate hardware, and poppies hand-painted by designer Kelly Bowman Greenwood make this playhouse something special.

RIGHT Pads cover the springs of the in-ground trampoline so that no one is injured by landing on them. The extra layer of turquoise pads protects kids who jump out of the trampoline area.

FAR RIGHT Older children and parents can sit close enough to watch the action and enjoy the warmth of an outdoor fire.

C hildren's play structures are incorporated seamlessly into this well-designed backyard. A large Connecticut Bluestone patio is the main hangout area of the garden, surrounded by a low stone wall used for extra seating. Parents sit here by the fire and watch their children play nearby. Landscape designer Kelly Bowman Greenwood selected throw pillows that would tie together colors used in planting beds and on the playhouse.

A flagstone path provides a graceful entrance to the playhouse and branches off to an arbor covering a secluded wooden bench. On the opposite side of the backyard is an area of artificial grass that never needs to be mowed or watered and stays green year-round. Because mature trees in this backyard block a large amount of sunlight from coming through, artificial grass was the only way to go. It beautifully frames a trampoline built into the ground so that children will land on a level, soft surface if they accidentally miss the bouncy center.

The Elements

- **Play structures:** Playhouse kit with artistic accessories and custom paint; in-ground trampoline.

- **Hardscaping:** Connecticut Bluestone patio with brick border; flagstone paths; South Bay quartzite ledge stone wall with an Arizona flagstone cap.

- **Landscaping:** Artificial grass; shade-loving ferns, ground covers, flowers, and shrubs.

- **Accessories:** Wood-burning fireplace; potted plants; colorful throw pillows; candles; birdhouses.

Natural Wonderland

There are many curves and circles in this design that lead people smoothly from one destination to the next.

OPPOSITE PAGE, TOP
Patterned concrete stepping-stones lead through a maze of touchable plants.

OPPOSITE PAGE, BOTTOM
Bright kangaroo paws and soft lamb's ears are winners in every kid-friendly garden.

This backyard proves that you can have a beautiful landscape that is also friendly to children and pets. Landscape designer Katey Mulligan set out to create a space filled with interesting sights, sounds, textures, fragrances, and motions that would inspire imaginative play. There's enough grass to practice cartwheels or sit on a blanket reading a book, plus significant areas of mulch for the family dog to romp around in.

A simple tepee, impermanent and understated, sits beneath the shade of a cotoneaster tree. The children incorporate stepping-stones into their adventures, and they dart in and out of the ornamental grasses and shrubs. Another focal point of the garden is a terra-cotta spill fountain featuring cobalt blue recycled glass that has been tumbled to dull sharp edges. There is no standing water that might pose a safety risk, yet kids can still touch the water running down the sides of the urn. Around the elevated fountain are kid favorites such as fuzzy kangaroo paws, silky lamb's ears, and soft *Carex testacea* grass. This design will grow effortlessly with the children while providing adults with a rejuvenating retreat.

The Elements

- **Kid-friendly features:** Tepee; spill fountain; grass; concrete and flagstone stepping-stones; plants that spark the imagination; shade from a mature tree; arbor with climbing vines.

- **Animal-friendly features:** Wood-chip mulch; grass; nonpoisonous plants; shade from a mature tree.

- **Lighting:** Low-voltage landscape lighting around the paths; uplights in the cotoneaster tree; spotlight on the terra-cotta urn.

Chapter 6

Light and Heat

When you have a beautiful, well-designed backyard, you'll want to be outdoors practically every hour of the day. Make that possible by incorporating lighting, heating, and shade structures into your plan. Outdoor lighting is an art that's often best left to professionals, but we'll give you some basic design tips and ideas to think about. The soft glow of a fire provides light and heat at night and makes the backyard feel festive. During the day, you'll need protection from the sun, so consider all the options, from patio roofs to cabanas and umbrellas. Then you'll be ready to enjoy the space from sunup to sundown and beyond.

Backyard Lighting

Putting lights in multiple areas creates a soft glow across the entire backyard.

Landscape architects and contractors agree that it's best to hire a specialized outdoor-lighting designer to come up with a plan for your backyard. Choosing the right number of lights and wattage to ensure you have enough light outdoors—but not too much—can be tricky. While lighting for safety purposes is important, outdoor lights will also improve the view from indoors at night. Designers categorize lighting needs based on functionality (what's needed for safety) and accent (when lights are used to highlight a particular focal point).

Low Voltage

Landscape lighting used to be built on 120-volt systems and required an electrician to install, but now most people opt for low-voltage lighting that uses just 12 volts of electricity, making it possible to install yourself.

To power the outdoor lights, you'll need a transformer, which steps down the 120-volt current in your house to 12 volts. Before you can buy one, determine how many lights will be attached to it and what wattage those fixtures are. The transformer should handle the wattage needs you have now, plus about 25 percent more so it doesn't operate at full

ABOVE Large windows supplement outdoor lighting on a patio.

LEFT Aim lights up into a tree to highlight sculptural branches.

RIGHT Low-voltage lights can illuminate paths or groupings of plants.

capacity. If you might add more lights in the future, buy a transformer that can handle 50 percent more wattage. Then plug the transformer into a GFCI-protected outdoor receptacle and you're ready to go.

Layering your landscape lighting will give you the best overall effect. Start by lighting the perimeter of your garden so that you can see the boundaries from inside the house. Then light the paths, but do it artfully. "Never, under any circumstances, line a path with lights on both sides like an airport runway," warns William Morrow. Stairs should have their own light source if they aren't close enough to the porch light, so people don't trip. Finally, add some accent lighting to features you want to enjoy at night. Use an uplight fixture under a tree with particularly lovely branches, or a spotlight aimed at a piece of art. If you want to see the silhouette of an object but not the object itself, place a backlight behind it facing toward the house. To mimic the shadowing effect of the moon, hang a light in a tree.

LANDSCAPE DESIGNER
WILLIAM MORROW ON

Buying Outdoor Lights

It's worth the extra money to buy high-end fixtures. They will save you a lot of grief down the road, when the less expensive ones break or go out every time it rains. Also, start off with less lighting than you think you need. You can always add more later and use candles on tables for intimate lighting in the meantime."

Decorative Lights

For parties and holidays, use temporary lighting sources to dress up the backyard. Strung lights that plug directly into an outdoor receptacle come in a wide range of designs, from bare bulbs to colored lights to bulbs surrounded in perforated metal or even willow branches. Hang them under the eaves of the house, cluster them underneath an open umbrella, or string them around deck rails.

Open-flame sources such as candles, lanterns, and luminaries give off a soft and romantic light. Glass hurricanes surrounding candles will prevent the flames from going out, both on the table and when candles are placed atop stakes standing throughout the garden. Cast-iron and glass lanterns usually have real candles in them, though some run on gas. Either way, keep all open flames well away from plant foliage and make sure that lanterns set on tables and stakes are stable so they can't fall and catch a tablecloth or plant on fire.

Lighting Water

If you have a swimming pool or spa, you'll want to have light sources underwater. This is necessary for safety so people can see where the water is and avoid stepping into it, even if you don't plan to take any after-hours dips. Underwater lights also create a soft bluish green glow that makes the water look inviting from inside the house.

Light garden pools, fountains, and waterfalls so you can enjoy these features at night. Underwater plants and fish look best when illuminated from above, so you can simply add some low-voltage fixtures that point down around the perimeter of the pool. There are numerous ways to light waterfalls, fountains, and streams. For example, lighting streams from under the water makes them look magical but not particularly natural. Consult a lighting designer to get the look and feel you want.

LANDSCAPE DESIGNER
PATRICIA ST. JOHN ON

Patio Lights

Indoor lighting is very bright and doesn't blend well with low-voltage outdoor lighting. If the patio light outside your back door is already on house voltage, replace the bulb with a 25-watt silk-wrapped light bulb. This quick fix will make the light more relaxing and subtle like the rest of your outdoor lights."

TOP Adding lights under an umbrella makes it glow like a firefly.

BOTTOM Strung white lights and a hanging lantern illuminate the pathway under a trellis surrounded by carefully pruned trees.

OPPOSITE PAGE, TOP Hang colored paper lanterns from the trees to create a magical mood.

OPPOSITE PAGE, BOTTOM LEFT Select an unusual porch light to give your patio a little flair.

OPPOSITE PAGE, BOTTOM RIGHT Metal lanterns with frosted glass hold small votive candles. Combine these with potted plants for a memorable night-time centerpiece.

Backyard Heating

LANDSCAPE ARCHITECT
ROB PRESSMAN ON

Outdoor Fireplaces

"I like to put outdoor fireplaces up against a wall. It helps to break up the expanse and provides a good backdrop to the fireplace itself. I also do a lot of double-sided fireplaces that are freestanding, when the space allows. That way you can have two seating areas that benefit from the warmth and glow of the fire."

There's nothing like a true masonry fireplace to create the feeling of an outdoor room. Add a couple of cushioned chairs with ottomans, a throw blanket, a cup of tea, and a good book, and you're set for a relaxing evening under the stars.

Building a real fireplace with the necessary footings, firebrick-lined firebox, and chimney can make it an expensive proposition, especially when you factor in the finish materials, such as stone or decorative concrete. Position wood-burning fireplaces so they are not directly under low-hanging trees, and make sure there's a spark arrester on the chimney. Also check that smoke won't blow into a neighbor's yard.

If the expense and hassle of a wood-burning masonry fireplace are too much, consider a prefab unit. You can buy a gas-fired model, which is better for the environment. In front-vented models, the exhaust is released through slots in the face frame, so you don't need a chimney at all. Zero-clearance units can be framed and finished with stucco, stone, or tile. Others are stand-alone art pieces that don't need to be finished on site.

OPPOSITE PAGE Adding an outdoor fireplace lets you enjoy your patio almost year-round. This prefab box is capped with stone veneer.

TOP This stucco fireplace has a leaning chimney to avoid low tree branches.

BOTTOM Decorate the mantel of an outdoor fireplace much as you would inside, complete with candles and garlands.

Fire Pits

These low structures have the feel of a campsite fire. They can be practically any shape or size and can be faced with brick, stone, stucco, tile, or concrete. Some are built to burn wood, but most run on gas and feature fake logs, glowing coals, or even recycled glass.

Landscape architect Ken Coverdell warns that the heat generated from gas fire pits is usually minimal and that the mechanisms seem to have a high failure rate. "Just like everything else that lives outdoors, electrical components on lighter systems have a hard time surviving the elements. Make sure you get a warranty and maintain the unit annually," Coverdell says.

Chimineas

The least expensive way to add fire to your backyard is with a portable or freestanding unit. It can be made of metal, but the most popular version, called a chiminea, is made of clay. These three-legged pots are lightweight and easy to move around the patio. Wood-burning versions should have a spark screen for safety. You can get chimney extensions if you want to use it on a porch so the smoke vents out.

LANDSCAPE ARCHITECT
CRAIG BERGMANN ON

Positioning Heat Fixtures

In addition to keeping tree branches away from fireplace chimneys for safety reasons, make sure you don't put any delicate potted plants too close to the fireplace opening, or even too close to heat lamps and fire pits, as the heat can make them wither."

LEFT Build a low wall around a fire pit for extra seating.

RIGHT TOP This copper fire pit is light enough to move around the patio. Clear glass pieces covering the gas-lighter system reflect the fire.

RIGHT MIDDLE Flames dance over pieces of glass in this modern-style concrete fire pit.

RIGHT BOTTOM Chimineas come in many styles and sizes. This one has an etched design, while others are faced with colorful tiles.

This infrared heater is wired to the patio roof and keeps the outdoor kitchen area warm enough to prepare dinner on cold evenings. Two hanging lamps and directional spot lighting bring further comfort and warmth into the space at night.

Heat Lamps

Families with young children are sometimes concerned about incorporating a fire pit or fireplace. In these cases, another option that will keep you warm enough to stay outside past sundown is a heat lamp. Most portable stand-up patio heaters use propane. The top of the heater will have a cap that directs the warmth down, and one can usually heat an area of 15 to 25 square feet. "I prefer natural-gas-fired heaters because they don't often fail," says landscape architect Ken Coverdell.

An alternative to natural-gas heaters is infrared heaters. They can be wired to a 120-volt or 240-volt electrical system, and some can be plugged into an outdoor receptacle. Radiant heaters will warm objects and people instead of the surrounding air. Because of the intense and directed heat they supply, they need to be installed at least 8 feet above the ground. "Wire the radiant heat lamp into trellises and arbors and they'll sit at about the right height. Plus, when they can blend into what they're installed on, they don't become the focus of the area," Coverdell says.

Misters

If you live in an area that gets uncomfortably hot in summer, consider installing an outdoor mister. These systems have nozzles that generate a fine spray of water to cool you without getting you wet. There are many different misting applications, including fans that shoot mist out, pump and hose systems that you can attach to an overhead structure, and even umbrellas that have misters built in. Set up a system where there's seating that gets a lot of sun. It's more pleasant to feel the mist when you're lying on a lounge chair, though, than when you're sitting around a table eating lunch.

TOP Infrared heaters provide nearly instantaneous warmth for a modest electrical output. Many units can simply hook onto an overhead structure and plug into a standard electrical receptacle.

ABOVE LEFT Propane-powered patio heaters are often seen at restaurants with outdoor seating. Look for a model with wheels so you can move it to where it's needed.

ABOVE RIGHT A patio misting system like this one easily attaches to an overhead structure.

Shade Structures

It may not have been the trend 30 years ago, but we now know that spending too much time in the sun, particularly without sunscreen, is not healthful. So when you're coming up with a design for your backyard, think about including shade structures and other areas where your family can enjoy the fresh air without always being in direct sunlight.

Study the landscape and note where you have existing large trees. Try to create destinations or activity areas under them where appropriate to get some natural shade. This can cause planting challenges, as there are many species that won't survive at the base of a large tree. Sometimes hardscaping under these areas is the best way to go.

ABOVE A simple wooden structure with canvas stretched across the top provides a shady place to sit and have tea in the middle of the garden.

OPPOSITE PAGE, TOP LEFT Small portable umbrellas are ideal next to pools. This one uses a planted pot as a base.

OPPOSITE PAGE, TOP RIGHT A spa in the shade of large trees may be harder to keep clean, but it will be more enjoyable to soak in.

OPPOSITE PAGE, BOTTOM A frosted-glass patio roof allows light to filter in but not become overwhelming.

Patio Roofs

If your patio is often in direct sunlight, building a shade structure that covers the area will allow you to enjoy the space any time of day. In general, south-facing patios get the most sun during the day, while west-facing patios get midafternoon sun. If your patio faces either of these directions, you'll want to consider adding some shade.

Be aware that large structures like these often require building permits to ensure that safety standards are met. There may also be zoning ordinances that indicate how tall and far back from your neighbor the structure needs to be. Check with your local building department during the planning stage to avoid any surprises or angry neighbors.

Spacing the overhead beams will provide some shade yet still allow sun to filter through. If you want to avoid sunlight altogether, either build a solid roof or train a vine to grow over the top of an open patio roof. Some of the best plants for this use are bougainvillea, wisteria, several species of clematis, and grape vines. Check with your local nursery to select a hardy vine for your area.

Gazebos

Gazebos are stand-alone structures that are generally placed farther out in the garden. They are destination areas where people can gather, sit in a shady spot, and feel like they are far away from home. Gazebos are available as kits, or you can custom-build one to match the style of your house. They are usually round and open on all sides, so you have a panoramic view of the garden.

OPPOSITE PAGE, LEFT Solid patio roofs can incorporate accessories that wouldn't hold up as well exposed to the elements, such as a candelabra and a wood-framed mirror.

OPPOSITE PAGE, RIGHT Woven bamboo shades attached to a simple overhead structure provide additional shade to a chic outdoor lounge.

ABOVE LEFT Beams spread far apart provide shade when the sun is rising and setting but not during midday.

ABOVE RIGHT A rustic bentwood gazebo adds timeless appeal to a mature yard.

LANDSCAPE DESIGNER
PATRICIA ST. JOHN ON

Patio Roofs

Pay attention to the sun pattern in your yard so that the patio roof or arbor you build shades the area you want. For one client I planted table grapes that climb up the arbor so people can pick clusters and eat them as they relax in the backyard."

Whether you're shopping for a simple table and chairs or several groupings of furniture for a large area, your main considerations should be style, comfort, and quality. It can be tempting to buy inexpensive outdoor furniture. You may reason that it's going to be outside and that it's therefore pointless to pay for quality when the furniture might get ruined anyway. In fact, buying inexpensive furniture will ensure that outcome. Low-quality materials and finishes won't stand up to the elements, and the pieces will end up in a landfill. You will save money in the long run if you buy well-made, long-lasting pieces, and it's the more eco-friendly choice as well.

"Placing nice-looking benches or groupings of tables and chairs throughout the garden is an unspoken invitation to enjoy the area," says landscape designer Patricia St. John. "The choice of furniture can go a long way to unify the look of the garden, so it's important to spend the extra money to perhaps carry out the style of the inside of the house and bring the whole thing together."

Materials and Finishes

Look for wooden furniture harvested from sustainably managed forests and constructed with mortise-and-tenon joinery. Marine-quality hardware and finishes will ensure that a piece won't rust or be damaged by water. While wicker furniture seems outdoorsy, it won't last in the backyard. Instead, opt for wicker look-alikes made

of a weatherproof resin that resists fading, cracking, and tearing. Metal furniture looks great outdoors, but it must be kept sealed so it doesn't rust.

Dining Tables

Particularly if you plan to eat outdoors on a regular basis, you'll want to select a table-and-chairs set that's comfortable for lingering meals and entertaining. Buy a table that seats at least eight people so that you have room for family members and friends. Larger tables that can accommodate platters of food for family-style meals also provide plenty of space for table settings. Choose a solid tabletop, rather than something with gaps or slits, so that spilled liquid doesn't end up in your lap. And if the table and chairs will be in direct sunlight, consider buying a table with a hole in the middle for a shade umbrella.

TOP LEFT A funky metal table-and-chairs set was given new life with a coat of bright blue paint.

TOP RIGHT These sea grass chairs surrounding a concrete table show that mixing materials can work beautifully.

ABOVE A grouping of outdoor chairs with purple cushions adds a punch of color to this otherwise woodsy backyard.

LANDSCAPE ARCHITECT
CRAIG BERGMANN ON

Choosing Outdoor Furniture

It's always a good idea to arrange actual furniture outside to see how much space you really have. But outdoor furniture is typically oversized, so be cautious. Also, the materials you choose need to relate to the architectural style of the house."

Cabanas

While gazebos are open on all sides, cabanas traditionally have three lightweight walls and one open wall facing a pool. Fabric is often used for the sides and can be tied back to allow a cool breeze in, or left down to block harsh sunlight. Cabanas don't have to be near a pool, of course. They're also great as a stage for kids to put on plays. The roof can be fabric or something more solid like wood shingle or even metal. A thatched roof will give the cabana a tropical feel.

LANDSCAPE DESIGNER
KATEY MULLIGAN ON

Outdoor Fabrics

I love to use outdoor fabrics that can fold up, like Roman shades for cabanas. Another great choice is bamboo or willow fabrics that can be tied up or to the side. For a more high-tech look, try fabulous metal mesh fabrics."

ABOVE LEFT
Concrete pillars
support a metal-
framed roof, making
this cabana look like
something you'd see
at a five-star resort.
Panels of curtains on
each side are available
to block sunlight as it
travels across the
backyard.

ABOVE Sheer curtains
surround a simple teak
base nestled among
tropical flowers and
hot-colored candles.

RIGHT Built-in
seating adds extra
functionality to this
wooden cabana.

Retractables

A retractable awning provides shade when extended but can also be out of the way, allowing sun to shine into the house. This gives you a lot of flexibility for different seasons. There are mechanized options, or you can rig something up with outdoor fabric. Simply install two rows of wire across the area you want to shade, sew grommets into the edges of the fabric, and pull the fabric across the wires with the end of a long pole as shown at left.

Shade Sails

These taut fabric canopies are stretched from three or more points and resemble the sail of a ship, especially when the wind picks up. Look for one made of a high-tech fabric that blocks ultraviolet rays. For large and non-square areas, shade sails are more economical than multiple umbrellas or a retractable awning. Their unique look also adds style and dimension to the backyard. Overlapping two or more shade sails can transform them from something functional into an artistic feature. "It's a dynamic way of creating shade, and it gives the space a ceiling, helping to define it as more of an outdoor room," says landscape architect Rob Pressman.

Umbrellas

Perfect for providing shade around a small dining area or two lounge chairs, umbrellas come in a rainbow of colors and patterns. Though cumbersome, they are movable. Bases can be tipped and rolled on their sides with the umbrellas removed. Long-lasting umbrellas that will withstand the elements and not tip over every time you walk by will cost a little more, but that extra money pays off in longevity and convenience. If you want an umbrella to simply shade a table, buy a table with a hole in the middle to hold the umbrella. That way, everyone has a good amount of shade when the sun is high in the sky.

OPPOSITE PAGE Panels of outdoor fabric pulled across wires block the sun from this outdoor game room.

TOP You can have fun designing with shade sails. Overlapping them like this creates the effect of a permanent floating kite in your backyard.

ABOVE A row of white umbrellas protects sunbathers lounging by the pool.

Porches

Attached to the back of the house with a solid roof, a porch is a natural extension of an indoor living space. As such, it is usually decorated like an indoor room, complete with upholstered furniture, throw rugs, and floor lamps. Particularly if your backyard is sheltered from wind, it's possible to have nice things out on the porch for most of the year and not worry about them getting damaged by sun or rain.

Bring the look of the garden onto the porch by adding potted plants. If the roof of your porch is low, brighten up the space with electric lights. In hot areas, installing a few ceiling fans will allow people to get some fresh air outdoors without getting stifled. Also consider wiring for outdoor speakers. Add a few rocking chairs or a swinging bench and you'll have created the preferred place to sit and enjoy dessert every night. In areas where mosquitoes are prevalent, screening in the porch will allow people to be outdoors without suffering.

LANDSCAPE DESIGNER
WILLIAM MORROW ON

Screened Porches

If the house or space allows for it, a screened-in porch is a must in the DC metropolitan area where I work. The aggressive Asian tiger mosquito has migrated up from the South and can make being outdoors a bloody experience. If the porch is large enough, just screen in part of it for a little relief."

ABOVE This conservatory is the perfect blend of indoors and out: Rustic furnishings are protected against the weather, yet potted plants and grapevines get all the sunlight they need through overhead glass panels.

LEFT Lightweight woven chairs, a bright-colored Moroccan table, and whimsical hanging stars are airy counterpoints to the traditional brass sconce, paneled wainscoting, and Persian rug in this small conservatory.

OPPOSITE PAGE This sunroom-greenhouse features an angled roof with clerestory windows to let in more light.

Sunrooms

Similar to porches, sunrooms or solariums can be attached to the house or may be freestanding, but they have windows instead of screens. With a sunroom, you get all the creature comforts of being inside (including heating and air conditioning) but with a panoramic view of the backyard. These glass structures are similar to greenhouses, which is why sunrooms are also great places to grow houseplants or start new seedlings.

English-style conservatories are more upscale versions of sunrooms and usually have glass panels on the roof as well. Sunrooms of all styles can either be constructed on site or put together from kits. Be sure you get energy-efficient glass with UV protection, and consider having one or more operable windows so you can get some fresh air if you'd like to. Sunrooms are generally constructed in an area that gets a lot of direct sunlight, so consider installing solar panels on the roof. It will give you a feeling of accomplishment to know that energy is being collected while you sit in the sunroom reading a book.

Keeping Warm

A backyard overlooking the Pacific Ocean would be a dream come true for almost any homeowner. To make the most of this one, landscape architect Ken Coverdell created a border of colorful plants to frame the view. Then he added a fire pit with plenty of seating so that the family could enjoy their surroundings even on cold and overcast days. Throw cushions make the low stone benches more comfortable, and the break in the middle ensures that no one is sitting with his or her back to the ocean.

A simple outdoor counter was built to one side of the fire pit with the same stone to unify the two areas. Coverdell chose a granite countertop for its durability, and he had a hole cut out on one end to make room for the family's charcoal barbecue. "The homeowner insists on using charcoal to cook and loves this barbecue, so we designed the counter around it," Coverdell says.

Before dinner, guests can get a closer look at the luscious landscaping by taking a leisurely stroll across the stepping-stone path. Then they can head back to the warmth of the fire pit to watch the sun set into the ocean.

Low stone benches with concrete tops surround a fire pit that's situated so that people can enjoy the stunning view.

TOP This simple stone counter with a long granite countertop has the dual purpose of providing a stable area for the cook to work on and a place for people to sit and eat.

BOTTOM A stepping-stone path borders the blooming plants and eventually leads through them to a closer view of a golf course between the backyard and the water.

The Elements

- **Fire pit:** Gas-fired, surrounded by stone-veneer benches that are topped with round-edged cast concrete.

- **Lighting:** Task lighting around the barbecue; low-voltage landscape lighting; lights built into benches around the fire pit.

- **Hardscaping:** Aggregate concrete patio; stone stepping-stones.

- **Outdoor kitchen:** Stone-veneer counter; granite countertop; charcoal barbecue.

- **Furniture and accessories:** Metal bar stools with padded cushions; colorful throw pillows.

All-Season Courtyard

The columnless patio cover provides shade without boxing the area in. To cover the structure, designer Jim Pollack used herringbone-patterned saguaro rib wood, which are the bones of a saguaro cactus that has died. To save space in this small courtyard, the wood-fired pizza oven was installed on top of the mesquite-burning fireplace. Native plantings and artwork add further interest to this courtyard.

The owners of this Tucson, Arizona, backyard asked landscape designer Jim Pollack to squeeze a fireplace, seating area, spa, outdoor kitchen, and wood-fired oven all into a 20-by-20-foot courtyard. "I told them, 'This is going to take me a while,'" Pollack says. "But once I began drawing it up, the elements fit into place perfectly."

Pollack used low curved walls to give the space a sense of movement and continued them in the design of the fireplace and patio ceiling. With the light of the fire on one end, lanterns on the home's adobe walls, recessed lights in the patio roof, and a spotlight next to the barbecue, this courtyard stays bright enough to enjoy late into the evening.

Gravel planted with natives such as succulents and cactus borders the stained concrete patio. Concrete also tops the low adobe block walls so they can double as extra seating. The materials, design, and lighting combine to create an outdoor room that is a true extension of the home.

The Elements

■ **Lighting:** Bulbs recessed into the patio roof and sconces on the exterior walls all tap into wiring from the house; spotlight on the barbecue grill; large windows and French doors allow indoor fixtures to illuminate the patio as well.

- **Heat:** Stacked wood-burning fireplace and pizza oven.

- **Shade:** Curved, columnless steel patio roof covered in saguaro rib wood.

- **Hardscaping:** Stained concrete patio bordered by gravel; low adobe walls with concrete caps.

- **Landscaping:** Natives such as Mexican fence post succulents, San Pedro cactus, golden columbine, autumn sage, and little leaf ash.

Chapter 7

Furniture and Accessories

With so many styles and materials to choose from, shopping for outdoor furniture can seem daunting. Just as with indoor furniture, you'll want to buy pieces that match the style of your backyard and that are comfortable and well made. If you have room, select a dining table that seats up to eight, plus have a few chairs or benches scattered throughout the backyard to encourage people to venture out into the garden. Then add finishing touches, such as pots and garden art, to make the backyard look homey or to emphasize a particular style.

Outdoor Furniture

Substantial wooden furniture with mortise-and-tenon joinery will last a long time.

Lounge Chairs and Cushions

"It's important to purchase comfortable furniture," says landscape designer William Morrow. "Don't skimp here. You are asking a lot of a piece of furniture to withstand exposure to the elements. If you buy quality, it will last 20 years." This advice pertains not only to tables and dining chairs but also to lounge chairs and side tables. Look for lounge chairs that are adjustable, and sit on them for a while in the store to make sure they provide support where you need it.

Just because you buy high-quality furniture doesn't mean you don't have to maintain it. Clean outdoor furniture regularly, keep it sealed, and don't leave cushions out in the rain. The best way to keep cushions clean is to store them in a garage or shed and bring them out for a few days or a week at a time when you know you'll be using them.

Today's high-performing outdoor fabrics offer more choices than ever. Not only do new materials stand up to water and UV rays, but they come in colors and patterns that are easy to decorate with. If you've incorporated low stone or concrete walls in your garden, buy 10 or so throw pillows and disperse them throughout the garden during parties. Put them on stairs and atop walls, and even out in the middle of the lawn, to add color and comfort.

CLOCKWISE FROM TOP LEFT Create seating areas around the garden as destination points.

These sleek metal lounge chairs are topped with a woven fabric that's easy to hose down.

Create a tropical look with punchy throw pillows and Balinese umbrellas.

Don't be afraid to use bright colors outside, especially those that appear in nature.

Just as they do indoors, bright and colorful throw pillows dress up a patio outdoors.

Outdoor Beds and Rugs

As children, we camped outside in sleeping bags and gazed up at the moon. The adult version is having an outdoor bed in the garden. As with cushions, it's best not to leave a bed exposed to the elements for months at a time. Bring the mattress out on weekends or whenever you entertain. That way, you can dress it up with sheets and pillows and not have to worry about bugs and mold.

Rugs tie seating areas together. Natural materials such as sea grass and sisal work well outdoors and have a texture that looks right on stone or concrete patios surrounded by plants.

ABOVE A bright orange rug offsets minimalist white lounge chairs.

OPPOSITE PAGE, TOP LEFT Raised off the ground, this red upholstered platform is a cozy place to sit and chat during parties.

OPPOSITE PAGE, TOP RIGHT This showstopping daybed is a posh shaded oasis of pillows for afternoon lolling.

OPPOSITE PAGE, BOTTOM LEFT Woven sisal or sea grass is an ideal material for an outdoor rug.

OPPOSITE PAGE, BOTTOM RIGHT Put a stack of washable cotton lap blankets outside when you entertain, so guests can stay warm outdoors.

Hammocks and Swings

If you like the idea of an outdoor bed but aren't quite ready to take on the maintenance and expense of one, consider a hammock. Attach both sides to something solid, such as two tree trunks or even eyebolts in walls, and you're ready for a midday nap. Or, if you want to put your hammock in an open area, you can get one with its own stand. The stands range from simple metal designs to carved wooden bases that are true works of art. Some people prefer hammocks that are made of a solid acrylic fabric, which won't mark your skin the way some open-rope hammocks will. When space isn't an issue, it's best to buy a hammock that's large enough for two adults or several children. Hammock swings allow you to sit up rather than lie down, and they support you on three sides.

OPPOSITE PAGE, LEFT This red-and-white acrylic fabric hammock is comfortable enough to spend an afternoon in it, getting lost in a book.

OPPOSITE PAGE, RIGHT An elegant crocheted hammock is perfectly suited to this classic covered porch.

ABOVE LEFT A sheet of outdoor fabric and some throw pillows add comfort and color to a standard rope hammock.

ABOVE RIGHT Hammock swings are just as comfortable as hammocks, and they require only one hanging point.

Decorating with Pots

Pots blooming with tropical plants accent a brightly colored stucco wall.

In the same way that you use pillows, throws, and vases of flowers inside, you can use potted plants as finishing touches out in the backyard. Instead of waiting for plants that grow in the ground to bloom, get instant gratification by buying a pot of flowers at their peak. When the blooms have faded, move the plants to another area of the garden where they will be relatively hidden during their dormant season. Next year, bring them out to center stage again.

On patios and decks where you can't plant in the ground, bring nature that much closer to the house with potted plants. If you have only hardscaped areas, such as in a courtyard, don't limit potted plants to low flowers. In addition, use large pots to make a statement with citrus trees and bamboo. Potted plants also make excellent space dividers. You can block the view of the spa area with tall horsetails in rectangular pots, or create a separate dining room with rows of shrubs. In the garden, pots can be used to lead visitors from one area to the next. Line paths with pots to direct traffic.

ABOVE Tall and narrow pots hold rounded conifers, resembling a row of ice cream cones.

RIGHT Blooming lavender surrounds a potted palm in a Mediterranean landscape.

BELOW Terra-cotta pots provide seasonal blooms around this raised spa.

Do you love a plant that doesn't traditionally grow well in your area? Because pots are portable and you can fill them with whatever type of soil you want, they allow you to grow almost any plant and then move it indoors or to a greenhouse during times of year when it wouldn't otherwise survive.

Even a pot without plants can make a statement in the backyard. Create a grouping of different-sized pots, mix terra-cotta and ceramic, or paint pots a few bright colors and use them as decorative accents.

THIS PAGE, CLOCKWISE FROM LEFT When you're choosing container plants, remember that they can go down as well as up.

Pots can also add texture to a garden. This pot has a combed clay exterior and a spiky plant.

As a centerpiece, use upside-down pots that elevate candles.

Pots can look beautiful without plants, either empty or filled with water. Just remember not to leave standing water in the garden when mosquitoes are looking to lay eggs.

Potted cactus in slightly varying pots get plenty of sun on an outside sill.

OPPOSITE PAGE Groupings of pots don't need to have matching plants. The lowest pot here has a neat flattop of woolly thyme, while the other two hold lavender and bougainvillea to match the surrounding landscape.

OPPOSITE PAGE Hanging metal bells have an ethereal look and make a soft chiming sound when the wind picks up.

ABOVE Scatter garden art around the edges of a deck or patio as a finishing touch.

LEFT Sculptures are a great way to add style to the garden.

RIGHT This eagle-and-bear totem was carved from a salvaged cedar log. Rounded and weathered, it rises above a cluster of native Western sword ferns.

Make the backyard your own by adding art and finishing touches that say "home" to you. Incorporating art is also a great way to emphasize a particular style that can be punctuated with your choice of plants and hardscape.

Take cues from the architectural style of your home. A Western ranch house with adobe walls and a sloping roof would go well with rustic metal sculptures or bright Spanish-style tiled objects. A cottage-style house might have a collection of birdhouses surrounded by wildflowers. If your home has no particular architectural style, the sky is the limit. You might create a tropical paradise with hanging lanterns and tiki torches, or an Indonesian-style hideaway with statues, Zen fountains, and bold-colored flowers.

When you have a particularly special piece of garden art, give some thought to where you want to install it. It should be a focal point with at least one path leading to it that entices people to get a closer look. Make sure the art can handle the weather in your area, and protect it from rust and damage.

LANDSCAPE DESIGNER
KATEY MULLIGAN ON THE

Element of Surprise

Think of ways to incorporate art and garden decor in unexpected ways. "I like to install doors that don't lead anywhere but suggest that there's something on the other side. The door can even open, and you can have a surprise behind it, like a mirror, which makes the space seem larger and more magical."

OPPOSITE PAGE, TOP Create something unique with salvaged materials that don't need to be long-lasting solutions, such as this old movie billboard hooked to a wooden frame. It looks perfect over a salvaged couch that's been transformed into an outdoor daybed.

OPPOSITE PAGE, BOTTOM This rusty old cast-iron tub now serves as garden art and a place to wash the family dog. The inside was painted green to match the surrounding foliage.

Found Objects

Landscape architect Craig Bergmann says that recycled objects are the inspiration for most of his gardens. "I like objects with age and scale, since the outside world is so much larger," Bergmann says. "Surface textures of old things are wonderful to contrast with plant materials. The bigger the object, the better the statement."

Incorporating recycled materials into your garden design is an environmentally friendly approach to creating a space that's uniquely your own. Search for treasures at local salvage yards and Goodwill stores, or search online for relics that may be past their prime. When you find something that inspires you, even if it isn't an object that's usually found in a garden, snap it up and see what you can do with it. Almost any container can be used as a planter if you drill a couple of holes in the bottom. Old wine barrels and metal tubs are often put to use this way. You can also use pots and pans and even old shoes. Architectural salvage, such as shutters or stone pillars, can lend a sense of permanence to a grouping of plants. Old single-pane windows that weren't energy efficient in their original purpose can be hung from the edge of a patio roof to frame a particularly lovely view of the garden. Once you start hunting around, you'll see why using recycled materials as outdoor art has become so popular.

ABOVE An old bathroom mirror hangs on the side of a house to reflect the view of the garden beyond, making the patio feel more like an indoor room.

LEFT A sculpted concrete finial adds an air of formality at the entrance of a patio.

BELOW An old wagon wheel simply leaning against a wall adds Southwest style to this courtyard.

Primary Colors

Primary colors—yellow, red, and blue—in the furniture and accessories reinforce colors found in nature and the hardscaping of this backyard.

OPPOSITE PAGE, TOP In an area used for meditation, comfortable throw cushions complement a tea station. The patterned blue and red area rug pulls the design together.

OPPOSITE PAGE, BOTTOM LEFT While this chair is away from the main seating area, a floral-printed red throw pillow visually connects it.

OPPOSITE PAGE, BOTTOM RIGHT Bright red chairs compete with red blooms, and tall bamboo blocks the dining area from wind, keeping the bold-print tablecloth in place.

The owners of this 15-foot-wide Southern California backyard asked landscape architect Rob Pressman to make the most of a small space by creating separate dining, living, and relaxation areas. They also wanted to use bold color, so Pressman selected plants that would work as a backdrop for bright accessories, with just a few blooming additions such as scarlet geraniums and abutilon.

A yellow stucco fireplace and low stucco wall define the outdoor living room. Concrete squares and grass combine to make an outdoor floor that is structurally stable yet alive. The raised terrace accommodates a small dining area, while behind the screen of podocarpus and surrounded by horsetail and bamboo is a secluded meditation area.

This backyard uses accessories normally reserved for indoors, such as pretty ceramic candleholders, pots, and vases. Comfortable furniture is spruced up with throw cushions, and flickering candles light the way from one area to the next. The key to making primary colors work in such a small space is to let one color play a dominant role while the others are used sparingly. In this example, the same hue of yellow is repeated throughout, followed by a lesser dose of red. Blue provides a sporadic accent.

The Elements

- **Furniture:** Teak chairs; powder-coated steel chairs in vermilion; side tables; dining table.

- **Accessories:** Candles; pillows; tablecloth; teapot; ceramics; rugs.

- **Hardscaping:** Wooden deck; concrete patio; concrete stepping-stones; low stucco wall; wood-burning fireplace.

Playing Dress-Up

Before and after pictures show the magic of accessorizing.

In just two weekends, this plain backyard was transformed into a cozy spot for entertaining. To start, the homeowners restored their Alaska cedar deck using a biodegradable cleaner, a power washer, and two coats of stain and sealer. A new strip of gravel between the deck and the lawn dresses up the area and makes mowing the grass a lot easier. A collection of circular concrete stepping-stones bought from a home improvement center adds a graphic element to the design.

Once the hardscaping was refreshed, the backyard became party ready in a matter of hours. Red paint gave a pair of old wicker chairs a quick face-lift. A variety of ceramic, terra-cotta, concrete, and metal pots were filled with plants of varying textures, colors, and sizes. As a final festive touch, a string of lanterns was stretched across one end of the deck, small candle votives were lit and placed on the steps, and larger candles in glass lanterns were hung under the green patio umbrella.

The Elements

- **Deck:** Alaska cedar.

- **Paths:** Crushed granite and concrete stepping-stones.

- **Lighting:** Strung and hung lanterns; candles; sconce light on an exterior house wall.

- **Furniture:** Round wicker chairs, metal table, patio umbrella.

- **Plants:** A variety of potted plants, including golden sweet flag (*Acorus*), blue fescue, rosy-bronze New Zealand flax, and silvery echeverias.

- **Accessories:** Throw pillows, metal art.

Chapter 8

Backyard Structures

Potting sheds, greenhouses, and cottages are adult versions of playhouses. These small structures built out in the yard allow you to forget about real life in the house and focus on growing plants, painting landscapes, or spending time with a good book. Backyard structures can serve as retreats in other ways as well, by giving in-laws or renters more privacy or by providing a home office that feels worlds away from laundry and dishes but that you can still access in your slippers. However you use them, backyard structures are truly a luxury.

Greenhouses

Having a backyard greenhouse is a dream for many avid gardeners. Greenhouses allow you to grow plants that might otherwise not survive in your climate, to more easily start seedlings, and to protect plants from the elements.

If you have some building skills, consider buying a greenhouse kit and assembling it yourself. Buy the largest greenhouse that will work in your space, as you'll most likely be able to fill it quickly. You'll have a choice of a wooden or metal-framed structure. Wood looks great but needs to be maintained to survive outdoors. If you choose a metal frame, make sure the manufacturer has included thermal breaks in the structure that keep the outside metal from conducting cold into the greenhouse.

You can also build a greenhouse of your own design, using recycled windows or polycarbonate sheets that attach to the frame. Polycarbonate is a strong material and is often preferred over glass, particularly on roofs. It's lighter than glass, and frosted polycarbonate diffuses light, which is beneficial for plant growth.

LEFT This 8-by-10-foot structure acts as a greenhouse and shed. The owner used old windows and a door that were salvaged from her house, but she decided against a glass roof because it would have been too hot in her climate.

TOP Inside the greenhouse/shed is a sturdy metal work-table that's easy to keep clean. A thick layer of gravel serves as a floor that can absorb spilled water.

BOTTOM LEFT The proper humidity for growing coleus seedlings is maintained under this antique glass bell.

BOTTOM RIGHT A polycarbonate-paneled greenhouse lets filtered light in, creating a warm and conducive area for growing seedlings.

Beyond the structure itself, you'll need to plan for electricity and plumbing. Have a landscape contractor bring power to the part of the garden where you plan to build the greenhouse, so that you can plug in heating and cooling devices if necessary. This will allow you to have grow lights or simple task lights in the greenhouse. If you want a misting or drip-irrigation system, you'll also need to bring water to the area. Or you may be able to use a long hose or tap into a nearby sprinkler head for your watering needs.

Just as with your home, you'll want to make sure the greenhouse is energy efficient so you don't lose any of your heated or cooled air. Depending on your climate, you might not even need a heating unit if the structure is sound. To save energy, add insulation to the north-facing wall and the floor, make sure the windows have double- or triple-thick glazing, and seal every air gap. Some greenhouses come with solar vent operators that will open to allow fresh air inside when the greenhouse gets too hot or humid. You can also add an exhaust fan to keep the greenhouse cool when needed.

TOP A sliding barn-style door makes it easy for a wheelbarrow to enter this potting shed.

MIDDLE Decorate the outside of your potting shed with antique garden tools.

BOTTOM A potting bench made of recycled wood and hand-painted with stencils sits in a corrugated metal structure with a polycarbonate roof.

OPPOSITE PAGE Doing double duty to support one side of an arbor, this potting shed is made of recycled materials and offers a protected place to work with plants.

Potting Benches and Sheds

When you enjoy gardening but aren't quite ready for a full greenhouse, potting sheds and benches are a good first step. Potting benches can be freestanding, placed against a storage shed, leaned up against the house, or covered by a shade structure such as a patio roof. When shopping for a potting bench, make sure that it's made of sturdy materials and that the bench is at the right height so you don't have to stoop to work at it. There should also be reachable shelves above the bench to hold gardening supplies. Having a hose nearby for cleaning off the surfaces and watering new plants will make things easier.

Potting sheds may simply be potting benches with a roof over them, or they can be small structures that function more like a shed (see pages 200–201) than a greenhouse. Because they aren't made of glass or polycarbonate, potting sheds aren't meant to have plants growing in them for long periods. They are simply work areas and a place to store garden supplies.

LANDSCAPE ARCHITECT
CRAIG BERGMANN ON

Logistics

When deciding where to put a greenhouse, consider areas of the garden that get shade in summer and sun in winter. "For both greenhouses and potting sheds, access to the driveway is important because you'll be hauling materials from the car. Make sure there's a path leading from the driveway to the structure that you can roll a wheelbarrow over."

Backyard Studios

OPPOSITE PAGE A blue barn-style door is the only part of this guest cottage that stands out among the foliage.

RIGHT Just steps from the main house, this stately in-law unit features the same brick siding and architectural details.

BOTTOM A small storage shed at the edge of the garden was converted into a home office. The white shutters, flower box, and rounded door with gate hardware give it a fairy-tale look.

Having a finished, enclosed structure in the backyard adds value to your house because it can be used in so many ways. A small 10-by-10-foot structure is perfect as a home office or a place to work on hobbies ranging from pottery to music. Larger studios with or without their own bathroom and kitchen can be used as guest cottages, rentals, or even a place for family members to live in for a while. If you have the space to build one and your local planning department allows it, you really can't go wrong by investing in a backyard studio.

Cottages

Once you have a guest cottage or in-law unit, you may suddenly be barraged with visitors. And you might not mind, since they will have their own private residence to retire to at the end of the day.

When you build a backyard cottage, you'll need to work with your local planning department to ensure that the structure conforms to any height limits and architectural design standards. There are also issues of easements and setbacks from property lines, as well as lot coverage limits that may affect what size cottage you can build. The structure must be built on a concrete footing and will need electricity and possibly running water and waste pipes, so the building process can be an expensive proposition. You may wish to hire an

architect to design the structure to match the style of the main house, particularly if the cottage will be nearby. If it's a little farther out in the garden or hidden behind mature plants, you might rather build something with its own distinct character. Whatever you decide, be sure to include plenty of windows so that people can enjoy the view of the garden.

Artist's Workshop

Whether you're a professional artist or simply enjoy painting, sculpting, or sewing in your free time, having space inside the house to spread out and make a mess is a luxury. Very few homes can afford the extra room, which is why building an artist's workshop in the backyard is an appealing option. Any fumes generated from your work won't make their way into the home, and for woodworkers, the dust, noise, and dangerous tools will be kept away from any children. Construct an artist's studio in a spot that gets natural light throughout the day, and design plenty of windows into the structure. Depending on your art, you may need electricity and water, so plan for them in advance.

Having a separate studio is also great for musicians. Whether it's for recording or for band practice, the studio keeps the noise away from the main house (though be sure you don't disturb any close neighbors). Insulate the walls, floor, and ceiling, and put in double-pane windows.

Home Office

More and more people are working from home every year. For some, being just steps from distractions like dirty laundry and dishes, or in view of children who are in someone else's care, makes it difficult to concentrate on the task at hand. Or you may simply not have an extra room that can accommodate the space you need, perhaps for an oversized drafting table, a reference library, or product samples. Building a cottage in the backyard gives you a space of your own and helps create a psychological break between home and work. Any home office should have comfortable furniture, a well-thought-out lighting plan, ergonomically correct heights for chairs and desks, and temperature control. If you plan and design the office well, you'll get much more done in the backyard than you did inside the main house—and you still won't have to get dressed for work.

TOP White walls, a concrete floor, tall French doors, and skylights are all elements that contribute to a minimalist yet functional artist's studio.

MIDDLE AND BOTTOM This architect's studio also serves as a test case for an environmentally friendly roof. Inside, the work surfaces and storage areas are designed for maximum efficiency. The countertops are made of wood salvaged from a bowling alley.

OPPOSITE PAGE A lush ground cover and climbing vines make this backyard cottage practically disappear into the garden. Once inside, the homeowner has prime views, thanks to plenty of double-hung windows.

LANDSCAPE DESIGNER
WILLIAM MORROW ON

Incorporating Backyard Structures

Whatever the purpose of the backyard cottage, be sure you put a lot of thought into the design of the structure. Plants can only do so much to hide something that doesn't look quite right in your garden. The safest bet is to keep with the architecture of the house."

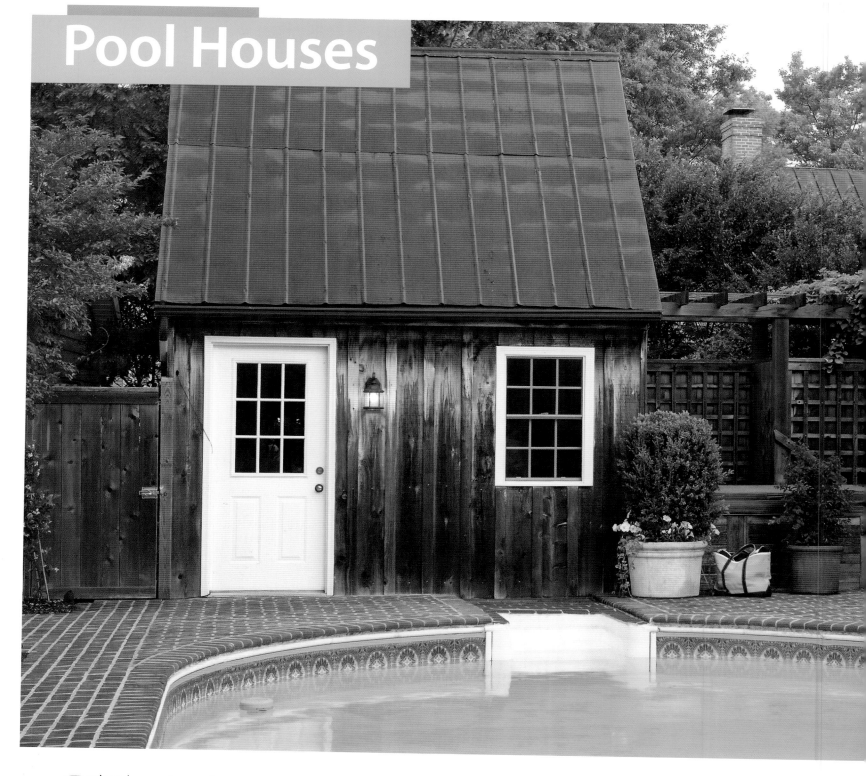

Pool Houses

Swimming pools require an enormous amount of equipment to run and maintain. Particularly in a large yard where the pool may be far from the house or garage, it makes sense to build a separate structure to contain all of the needed accessories. It can be a simple shed that's only big enough for the equipment, or you can take the opportunity to build a multipurpose building.

There are other reasons to build a poolside structure, including having a protected place to sit and enjoy the pool,

an area where guests can change into swimsuits and shower, and a place to entertain. Plus you won't have to deal with people tracking water and wet towels through the main house. You may even decide to build a guest cottage right next to the pool, complete with a bathroom and kitchen, to address poolside needs and to accommodate overnight visitors.

As with other backyard cottages, it's a safe bet to match the architectural style of the pool house to that of the main house, especially when the structures are close to each other.

LEFT This modest-sized poolside structure matches the style of the main house and is visually connected to it by the surrounding fence.

TOP A two-story pool house makes the most of a small space. Downstairs, the bathroom and storage space are easily accessible. Upstairs is a summer guest room.

BOTTOM An open-air pavilion allows you to enjoy the view of the water while lounging or dining outdoors, without being in direct sun. This elegant example has two bathrooms and a storage area.

Sitting at the edge of the water, most likely reflecting in the water as well, a pool house can provide a focal point in the garden. Inside, choose a floor that's easy on bare feet, that's slip resistant, and that won't be damaged by daily doses of water. Slate is a good choice, as are teak duckboards and ceramic tiles that have a bit of texture on the surface. If you have the space, building two or more changing rooms will come in handy for entertaining. Find at least one wall for rows of hooks that you can hang towels and wet bathing suits on.

Is your side yard or backyard full of lawn and garden accessories, tools, sports equipment, or kids' toys? Is your garage already at its limit with boxes, holiday decorations, and cars? When you've run out of storage space in the house and garage and the backyard is becoming a repository for everything you don't have room for, it's time to think about a storage shed.

Style and Function

There are several options and styles to choose from, depending on your needs, the design of your house and backyard, and what you plan to store. A simple lean-to shed has a sloping roof and generally sits against the side of the house or garage. It's great for hiding trash cans and storing a few landscape tools. Freestanding sheds are available in gable, saltbox, gambrel, and hip-roof styles. At your local home improvement center, you can find kits that are relatively easy to put together. These can be dressed up with paint and trim to match your house.

Or you may prefer a shed that has its own personality. You can create something unique by selecting old windows, doors, siding, and hardware from a local salvage yard. It's sometimes possible to find old roof shingles that are still in good shape, but if you can't, it's best to choose new materials that you know will be watertight. One relatively inexpensive and easy-to-install roof is corrugated or standing-seam metal panels that snap together. Another option for recycling is to use a playhouse that your kids have outgrown, particularly if the front door can be made larger.

If your goal is to store large sports equipment or a riding mower, you'll need a shed door that can accommodate it. Sliding barn doors will let the largest items through with ease. Also think about the path leading up to the shed. Make sure it's stable and sturdy enough to walk across when you're carrying large items, or to roll a wheelbarrow or stroller over.

Classic Shed

In summer, delphinium, salvia, and other perennials add punchy color.

OPPOSITE PAGE An espaliered tree grows against the side of the garden shed.

Landscape architect Craig Bergmann created period-appropriate gardens around this 19th-century suburban Chicago home. In the backyard he designed a dooryard cutting garden between the house and a restored garden shed. The shed itself matches the main house, with its white-painted siding and wood-shingle roof. A lattice fence connects the two structures. While designed to look like the house with its single black door, the back of the shed has double doors to accommodate a wheelbarrow and a lawn mower.

Bergmann planted orderly beds with annuals and perennials that offer colorful blooms for much of the year. A path of wood-chip mulch makes everything in the garden easy to reach and tend to. A rustic birdhouse perched on a white post lends some whimsy to the geometric design.

The Elements

- **Backyard structures:** Restored garden shed; latticework fencing; straight fencing with post caps; low garden gate.

- **Hardscaping:** Wood chip path; brick path.

- **Accessories:** Birdhouse.

Chapter 9

Getting It Done

Now that you've had time to dream, you're ready to think about the nuts and bolts of putting a plan on paper and getting the work done. Depending on the scope of your backyard remodel, you may want to hire professional help. Don't be afraid to call on a landscape designer for a consultation or even just a few hours of advice on a small project. This will most likely save you money and time if the designer is able to select plants that will survive in your backyard. Large projects will require the same kind of planning, time, and budget as most interior remodeling jobs.

Getting the Work Done

For anything other than adding a few new plants and perhaps incorporating a fountain or stepping-stone path, you'll most likely want to hire professional landscape designers and contractors. Consider how many elements you're changing and what site conditions will make those changes challenging to accomplish. Then think about whether you have the time to take on the design and construction yourself. In certain cases, you may need the services of a landscape architect.

Hiring Help

Landscape designer Kelly Bowman Greenwood suggests doing your homework before calling professionals for quotes. "Know what your issues are with the site and what new elements you want to incorporate so you can choose the right person for the job," Greenwood says.

So who is the right person for the job?

LANDSCAPE DESIGNERS are experts on which plants will do best in your area, so they can make shopping trips to the nursery much more productive. Some can also point you to the best local landscape contractors and even supervise their work. If your backyard remodel consists mostly of new plants and some hardscape elements such as a new patio and arbor, and if your site is currently in good shape, then a landscape designer will be the best option. Most are willing to work on small projects and charge by the hour.

LANDSCAPE ARCHITECTS must have a degree from a university and be licensed by the state to design complex landscapes. When you have challenging site issues such as a steep slope, or if you need retaining walls or drainage systems incorporated, you'll need to work with a landscape architect to meet local building codes in some cities. Where that isn't required, landscape

LANDSCAPE DESIGNER PATRICIA ST. JOHN ON THE

Benefits of Hiring Professionals

While it may cost more up front, hiring a professional to design your backyard so it will meet your needs for years to come pays off in the long run. "Because professionals have been exposed to hundreds of gardens, they know the best material options and how spaces can be laid out most effectively. They can also guide you on the best plant choices in your area and know where the plants will thrive in a water-efficient way."

architects are still good to have on your side, especially if your plans need to go through a difficult review for permits. Choose someone who has been working in the area long enough to know the process where you live and how best to navigate it. Most landscape architects tend to charge by the hour.

LANDSCAPE CONTRACTORS get into the nitty-gritty of the installation. They either do the labor themselves or have a team that will install anything from sprinkler and drip systems to patios and decks. They can bid on the project after looking at plans that your designer or architect has drawn up, or give you an hourly rate.

LANDSCAPE LIGHTING DESIGNERS specialize in putting together well-thought-out and energy-efficient outdoor lighting plans. You may find a landscape designer or architect who can design the lighting plan for you, but if you're working on your own or if lighting isn't something that your designer can take on, you can hire this part of the job out to a separate expert. Landscape lighting designers charge by the hour.

Interviews and Contracts

There are several reasons why it's important to look at some of the previous landscapes a designer has created. First, it will give the designer a chance to tell you about the scope of those projects so you can match your needs with what the designer has done.

It will also give you a chance to see whether the designer tends to work in a particular style. If all the pictures he or she shows you incorporate certain themes or materials, you'll likely get the same look. Simply find a designer whose style you like. If the portfolio

contains many different garden styles, it's likely an indication that the designer is willing to follow the vision of the homeowner. If you have a vision, this may be what you want. If not, it could end up being a frustrating relationship. "Trust your instincts," says landscape

LEFT The homeowners wanted to incorporate a pool and a raised spa on this backyard slope, so they hired a landscape architect.

RIGHT Landscape designers use plants to create an overall color scheme and mood in the garden.

designer William Morrow. "Design is a very personal thing, and you have to have a good connection."

Once you've met with several designers or architects, have seen their previous work in pictures or in person, and have spoken to their references, you'll be ready to draw up a contract. The contract should clearly spell out what the professional will be doing for you and include a time frame for when the work will be completed. Most landscape designers and architects will ask for a retainer to start the project. If they charge hourly, you may want to put a cap on the total number of hours they can bill for during each stage of the project.

Landscape contractors often suggest a fixed price for a project when they have time to work through a bid using final drawings. Sometimes it may seem like you'll save money by working on a time-and-materials contract, whereby the contractor bills you per hour and also gets reimbursed for any materials purchased. But this arrangement can backfire if something unexpected comes up, such as an old concrete slab that's harder to remove than expected, or if the soil is denser than anticipated and takes more labor to dig through. If you sign a fixed-price contract, these surprises won't change the budget numbers in the middle of the project.

Budget

When you meet with landscape architects and designers, they will likely ask what your budget is. It's possible that you won't know the answer to that question, but they should be able to guide you if you give them a general scope of work. If you do have a number you can't go beyond, you may need to refine the plan by eliminating something or choosing less expensive materials, but do not skimp on the functionality of the plan. It's also possible to create a plan for what your backyard will ultimately look like, then install it in stages as you are able to finance the work.

Another way to save money is to hire a landscape designer who is still in school or has recently graduated. You can find a landscape architect who hasn't yet been accredited by the state and will charge less per hour. This is usually a win-win situation in that you get a better price and you're giving a

LEFT Taking the time to plan every detail is even more important in small spaces.

RIGHT Retaining walls will require a building permit to ensure that they are constructed correctly.

Drawing Up Plans

Just as with interior remodeling projects, you'll need a drawn plan of the alterations you want to make to your backyard. Start by looking for a plot plan that shows your existing house and property lines. This plan usually accompanies the deed to your house. If it does not, your local planning department should be able to give you a copy and let you know about any building codes and ordinances that could affect your remodel. The plot plan can also make you aware of your property boundaries, easements, setback, and lot-coverage requirements.

From this plot plan, you or your landscape designer or architect can develop a base plan indicating the topography of the area, placement and size of buildings, location of everything from downspouts to fences and utility lines, large plants or trees that are staying, and any drainage problem areas. Once you have a working drawing, use it to map out ideas for new plants and hardscape, taking into account sun and wind patterns and how spaces will be used. A professional designer or architect can advise you on how much space each new element will take up, and make sure that plants are installed in areas where they will thrive. This part of the process can take weeks or months to complete.

Once you've made final decisions, a cleaned-up plan can be created to turn in to the planning department for permits, help you get material and labor quotes, and give you a clear picture of the end result. Don't move ahead with the construction until you're happy with the plan. It's much less expensive to go a few more rounds on the design than it is to change your mind once plants have been purchased and patios have been poured.

new professional something to add to his or her résumé. It's possible that things might not go as well or that you won't be as sure about what the final result might be, but it's just as possible that the designer will work extremely hard to make you happy as an initial client.

Getting Permits

Visit your local planning department during the design phase to make sure you are following all rules and regulations. Depending on the scope of the project, you may need one or more building permits. Rules vary from place to place, but in general, you will need a permit for any wall above a certain height; any structure, such as an arbor, attached to the house; any grading and drainage work; or any major project like a swimming pool.

Sometimes permits trigger other things that might not have been on your original wish list. "For example, if you're doing permitted construction, some cities require a soil test," says landscape architect Ken Coverdell. "It's not necessary to do a soil test when you're building a path, but when you're installing a new pool, it is important."

It's a mistake to think of permits as something you should try to get out of. Yes, there are fees associated with

permits, but when an inspector comes to your house to look at construction being done, he or she is concerned about your safety and the environmental effects of the work. The inspector may even find a problem that could save you time and money in the long run, such as pipes that don't have the right slope or a wall that's not structurally sound. Working with your local planning department will help make your project safe and legal.

Safe Digging

Before digging even a shallow ditch in your yard, confirm that there are no buried electric or gas lines. Every area has a local number to call to ask if these lines run in your yard. Search online for the number, and give them about 48 hours' notice to check the situation and get back to you before you start digging."

OPPOSITE PAGE
Dry-stacked stone walls match the rustic look of a cast-iron wood-burning fireplace.

RIGHT Lamb's ears and ornamental grass wrap around a terra-cotta pot.

Site Preparation

Even when you're just putting in new plants, landscape projects generate a lot of debris. If you hire a landscape contractor, he or she will be responsible for getting rid of it. Make sure this is done in the most environmentally friendly way possible. If you have a lot of soil to remove from the site, post an ad on the Internet and you'll likely find someone who will come to your home and pick it up to use in another project. This is less expensive, and more eco-friendly, than hauling it to the landfill. The same thing can work with rocks, boulders, and broken concrete. If you have wood from a tree that had to be removed, try to find a local business or furniture maker who could use the wood. If you must rent a debris box from your local waste-collection agency, make sure the materials will at least be recycled.

Protecting Existing Plants

Heavy equipment and machinery can do great harm to existing tree roots by compacting the earth and restricting the amount of water that can reach them. Protect your trees before construction begins by fencing off an area around each tree's dripline or a few feet beyond. The dripline is the circumference of a tree around its outermost branches.

If there's no way to block off the area around a tree, you can relieve root suffocation after the fact by renting a soil auger and filling the holes it creates with mulch mixed with fertilizer. This will allow water and air to reach the roots beneath the compressed soil.

Wheelbarrows and workers' foot traffic can tear apart a good-looking lawn in a matter of days. Protect a lawn that you want to keep by laying plywood boards across the grass and keeping people on that path. Fragile shrubs can be fenced off, or pulled out of the way with mesh or fabric sheeting. Just don't use plastic to protect plants, because hot air won't be able to escape and your plants will slowly cook.

Irrigation

No landscape plan is complete without an irrigation map. It's a costly mistake to plant new things if you won't have a working sprinkler or irrigation system from day one to keep them alive. Your designer or contractor will be able to advise you on the best system for the plants in your backyard. This can be a time-consuming part of the planning and installation, but it is crucial to the success of your landscape. The water needs of each plant, plus site considerations like sun, wind, and drainage, must be taken into account. If you chose plants carefully, the irrigation system won't be as hard to manage, because plants with similar water needs will be placed near one another. Try to use drip irrigation rather than sprinkler systems, as drips waste far less water through overspray and wind. Drip emitters put small amounts of water right where it's needed most, at the roots of each plant.

Timing

It's easy to get impatient, both during the design phase and while watching the construction unfold. Landscaping projects are just as likely to experience delays as interior remodeling projects. Common problems include ordering materials late, waiting for back-ordered materials to come in, and scheduling conflicts. But unlike interior projects, you also have to work around the weather. Rain, wind, extreme heat, and snow can all cause delays that no one can control. Try to schedule the work during a time of year when weather is less likely to be a factor, and then try to roll with the punches. "It takes time to plan and install a project," says landscape architect Craig Bergmann. "Do not be impatient. When things seem to be moving slowly, look again at your designer's finished work to remind yourself how well it will come together when the vision has the time to be realized."

Resources

The following are organizations, manufacturers, and retailers mentioned in this book along with a variety of others you might find helpful in creating your new backyard—with an emphasis on companies dedicated to environmentally responsible manufacturing processes and/or products.

Organizations and Associations

American Society of Landscape Architects
www.asla.org

The Association of Pool & Spa Professionals
www.apsp.org
703-838-0083

Association of Professional Landscape Designers
www.apld.com

Building Materials Reuse Association
www.buildingreuse.org
800-990-2672

Forest Stewardship Council
www.fsc.org
Non-profit organization established to promote the responsible management of the world's forests

Outdoor Kitchens

Barbeques Galore
www.bbqgalore.com
Barbecues and accessories

Dacor
www.dacor.com
800-793-0093
Outdoor appliances

Fogazzo Wood Fired Ovens and BBQs
www.fogazzo.com
866-FOGAZZO (364-2996)

Lynx Professional Grills
www.lynxgrills.com
888-879-2322

Marvel Refrigerators
www.marvelscientific.com
Outdoor refrigerators

Mugnaini
www.mugnaini.com
888-887-7206
Pizza ovens

Syndecrete
www.syndecrete.com
Concrete slab countertops

Vetrazzo
www.vetrazzo.com
Recycled glass countertops

Viking
www.vikingrange.com
888-VIKING1 (845-4641)
Outdoor appliances and
accessories

**Weber-Stephen
Products Co.**
www.weber.com
800-446-1071
Outdoor appliances and
accessories

Outdoor Furniture and Accessories

Allsop Home Garden
www.allsopgarden.com
866-425-5767
Solar lanterns and garden art;
garden tools

Ballard Designs
www.ballarddesigns.com
800-536-7551
Outdoor cushions and rugs

The Blue Rooster Company
www.thebluerooster.com
800-303-4312
Chimineas

Restoration Hardware
www.restorationhardware.com
Outdoor furniture and umbrellas

Shade Sails
www.shadesails.com
Tensioned fabric canopies

Smith & Hawken
www.smithandhawken.com
800-940-1170
Outdoor rugs, furniture, and
accessories

Sunbrella
www.sunbrella.com
Outdoor fabric

Whit McLeod
www.whitmcleod.com
707-822-7307
Outdoor furniture made of
recycled wood

Outdoor Activities, Structures, and Materials

**All-Safe Pool Safety
Barriers**
www.allsafepool.com
800-786-8110
Pool fences, safety net pool
covers

Aurora Deck Lighting
www.auroradecklighting.com
800-603-3520

Backyard Sports Center
www.backyardsportscenter.com
319-329-9382
Backyard court and net systems

Close the Loop
www.closetheloop.com
866-629-8414
Rubber mulch

Diamond Safety Concepts
www.diamond-safety.com
800-842-2914
Rubber flooring products

Greenhouse Kits
www.greenhousekit.com
877-718-2865
Lots of greenhouse styles,
materials, and accessories

**La Petite Maison
Playhouses**
www.lapetitemaison.com
877-404-1184
Custom playhouses and
doghouses

Pennington Seed
www.penningtonseed.com
800-285-SEED (7333)
SmartSeed lawn requires less
water

Practical Folly Playhouses
www.practicalfolly.com
905-658-0915
Whimsically styled playhouse
kits

Rainbow Play Systems
www.rainbowplay.com
800-724-6269
Wooden swing sets

The Safe Sand Company
www.SafeSand.com
415-971-1776
Silica-free sand

Screen Tight
www.screentight.com
800-768-7325
Porch screening systems

Springfree Trampoline
www.springfreetrampoline.
com
866-899-7370
Trampolines with hidden
springs; enclosures

SYNLawn
www.synlawn.com
866-796-5296
Synthetic lawn

TimberTech
www.timbertech.com
800-307-7780
Composite decking

TreeHouse Workshop, Inc.
www.treehouseworkshop.com
206-782-0208
Custom tree houses

Trex Co.
www.trex.com
800-289-8739
Composite decking

Credits

Photography

Simon Jonathan Webb/Alamy: 175 right; Jean Allsopp and Harry Taylor: 158; Caren Alpert: 84 top; Backyard Adventures of Colorado (www. playnix.com): 126 middle right; Robert J. Bennett: 116 bottom right; Allison Brown/Big Stock Photo: 67 bottom; Sue Scarfe/Big Stock Photo: 67 top; Laurie Black: 41 bottom right; John Keller/Blackline Fence Products: 66;

Paul Bosquet: 133 top left; Melanie Acevedo/Botanica: 10 bottom left; Marion Brenner: 19 bottom right; Rob D. Brodman: 9 bottom right, 10 top left, 10 bottom middle, 19 top left, 20, 22 bottom, 27 top, 46, 53 bottom right, 83 top middle, 83 top right, 87 bottom right, 129, 133 bottom, 143 top, 147 top, 170 bottom right, 171 bottom left, 173 top left, 177 top right,

178 middle right, 181 bottom left, 206, 211 top right; Linda Oyama Bryan: 202, 203 top right; Karen Bussolini: 199 bottom; courtesy of Barbara Butler: 119; Andrew Bordwin/ Beateworks/Corbis: 160 bottom; Jerry Harpur/Elizabeth Whiting & Associates/Corbis: 160 top; Tim Street-Porter/Beateworks/Corbis: 176; Eric Evans/Corner House Stock

Photo, Inc.: 3 left, 139; courtesy of Décor: 76 top left; Alan & Linda Detrick: 127; Ken Druse: 55 top right; Sergio de Paula/Fogazzo Wood Fired Ovens and BBQs (www.fogazzo.com): 76 bottom left; Roger Foley: 9 middle right, 12, 19 top right, 24, 25 top left, 25 top right, 25 middle right, 26, 32, 33 bottom left, 33 bottom right, 34 bottom left, 34 bottom right, 36, 37,

Design

2 left: Theresa Clarke Studio; 2 right: Huettl Thuilot Associates; 3 middle: Vermeil Design; 3 right: Richard Wm. Wogisch; 7: Theresa Clarke Studio; 8: P.O.P.S. Landscaping; 9 top right: Dean DeSantis, DeSantis Landscapes; 9 middle right: Michelle Murphy; 9 bottom right: Jim Lord Landscape Services; 10 top left: Jon Buerk, J. Buerk Landscape/Maintenance; 10 bottom middle: Mark Marcinik, Greenmeadow Architects; 11: Teri Ravel Kane; 12: Tom Mannion, Landscape Design; 14: Steve Morgan, Steve Morgan Landscape Architecture-Eco-Logical Design; 15 top right: Fung + Blatt Architects; 15 middle left: Paul Harris, Imagine Sonoma; 15 middle right: Jon Fernandez, JSF Company; 16: Joseph Marek, Landscape Architect; 19 top right: James David; 19 bottom right: Tina Beebe & Buzz Yudell; 20: Terry Mulrooney, Admiral Green Landscaping; 22 top left: The Fockele Garden Company; 22 bottom: Jon Buerk, J. Buerk Landscape/ Maintenance; 23: Michael Buccino, Michael Buccino Associates; 24: Scott Brinitzer Design Associates; 25 top left: James David; 25 middle right: Ryan Gainey; 25 top right: David Culp; 26: Raymond Jungles, Inc.; 27 top: Cathy Drees, Accent Gardens; 27 middle: Kendra Phelps and Norbert Kappel; 27 bottom: Richard Wm. Wogisch; 28: Phillip Sides Interior Design; 29: Griffith & Cletta; 31: Judy Kameon with Michael Kirchmann Jr, and Ivette Soler, Elysian Landscapes; 32: Oehme, van Sweden & Associates; 33 bottom left: Charles Stick; 33 bottom right: Sanchez & Maddux Inc.; 34 top left: Huettl Thuilot Associates; 34 bottom left: Scott Brinitzer Design Associates; 34 bottom right: Sanchez & Maddux Inc.; 36–37: William Morrow Landscape Design; 38 top left: Raymond Jungles, Inc.; 38 bottom middle: Anne Nichols; 39: Michelle Kaufmann Designs; 40: Pfau

Architecture; 41 top right: James Rowley, Naturally Beautiful Gardens; 41 bottom left: Tony Gwilliam; John Greenlee; 41 bottom right: John Breiling, (www.nwdecks.com); 43: Vi Kono, Creative Designs; 44 top right: Peter O. Whiteley; 44 top middle: Michael Manneh; 44 middle right: Julie Chai; 46: Jim Lord Landscape Services; 47 top: Scott Brinitzer Design Associates; 48: Jules Durant and Hendrikus Schraven, the Hendrikus Group; 49 top: Hillary Curtis, David Thorne Landscape Architects; 50: Stefan Thuilot with Joseph Huettl, Huettl Thuliot Associates; 51 top: Richard McPherson, Landscape Architect; 51 middle: Tony Gwilliam; John Greenlee; 51 bottom: James David; 52: Gary Marsh Design; 53 top left: Robert Glazier, Hill Glazier Architects and Andrew Glazier, Wild West Gardens; 53 bottom left: Raymond Jungles, Inc.; 53 bottom right: Vanessa Kuemmerle, Vee Horticulture; 55 top right: Ken Druse; 56: Peter O. Whiteley; 57 top: Nancy Driscoll; 57 bottom: Ryan Gainey; 58 bottom left: Jack Chandler & Associates; 59 top: Peggy Armand, Sanchez & Maddux Inc.; 59 bottom: Edwina von Gal; 60–61: Patricia St. John; 62–63: Katey Mulligan, Liquidambar Garden Design; 66: Carl and Lynne Steffens; 67 bottom: Luis Llenza Garden Design; 68 top left: Pamela Dreyfuss Interior Design; Exteriors Landscape Architecture; 68 top right: Simply Outdoorz; 68 middle left: Fine Landscapes, Ltd.; 68 bottom left: Deanna Glory Landscape Design (www.glorydesign.com); 69: Antonia Bava Architects; 70: Desert Sage Builders; 71 top: The Fockele Garden Company; 71 bottom: Desert Sage Builders; 72 top right: Desert Sage Builders; 73 top right: Buddy Rhodes Studios, Johnny Grey Kitchen Design; 73 bottom right: Janet Bell & Associates; 74 top right: Tom Ralston Concrete; 74 middle right: Karen Aitken & Associates; 75 top: Brian

Koch, Terra Ferma Landscapes; 75 bottom: Allison Rose; 76 middle left: Simply Outdoorz; 76 bottom left: Sergio de Paula, Fogazzo Wood Fired Ovens and BBQs (www.fogazzo.com); 77: Ransohoff, Blanchfield, Jones Inc. Landscape Architects; 78: Joe and Kalli Rivers Altieri; 79 top: Jeffrey Gordon Smith Landscape Architecture; 79 middle: Matthew and Joan Lane, Proscape Landscaping; 80: James David; 81 top left: Scott Brinitzer Design Associates; 81 top right: Jeffrey Gordon Smith Landscape Architecture; 81 bottom: Bill Hewett; 83 top right: Nicole Petersen, Kendell Mae's Kandlery; 84 top: Julie Chai; 84 bottom: Paul Hendershot Design; 85: Paul Hendershot Design; 86: Theresa Clark Studio; 87 top right: Landscape installation: Helmut Kroos Landscaping; 88 left: David C. Becker; 89 left: David C. Becker; 89 right: Brian Koch, Terra Ferma Landscapes; 90–91: Brian Koch, Terra Ferma Landscapes; 92–93: Hershberger Design; 95: Huettl Thuilot Associates; 96: Scott Brinitzer Design Associates; 97 top: Raymond Jungles Inc.; 97 bottom: Luis Llenza Garden Design; 98 top: Richard Wm. Wogisch; 98 bottom: Theresa Clark Studio; 99: Robert Norris; 100 top right: Clyde Timmons/DesignWorks; 100 middle right: Tom Mannion Landscape Design; 101: P.O.P.S. Landscaping; 102: Four Dimensions Landscaping Company; 103 top: Cevan Forristt Design; 103 middle: Desert Sage Builders; 103 bottom: Scott Brinitzer Design Associates; 104: David Deakin and Kathy Vannozzi, Deakin + Vannozzi Landscape Design; 105 bottom left: Hillary Curtis, David Thorne Landscape Architects; 105 bottom right: Raymond Jungles Inc.; 106: Bernard Trainor + Associates; 107 top: Michael Stusser and David Stucky; 107 middle: Robert Glazier, Hill Glazier Architects; Andrew Glazier, Wild West Gardens; 107 bottom: Chris Rosmini Garden

Design; 108 left: Kathleen Shaeffer, Great Gardens; 108 right: Bill Hewett; 109 left: Scott Brinitzer Design Associates; 109 right: Desert Sage Builders; 110–111: William Morrow Landscape Design; 113: Sasha Tarnopolsky, Dry Designs; 114: Home Place Structures; 115 top: Home Place Structures; 115 bottom: The Fockele Garden Company;116 bottom left: EDI Architecture; 119: Barbara Butler, 121 top right: Clemens & Associates, Inc.; 124 bottom: Jack Chandler, Landscape Design; 125: Derviss + Chavez Design + Build; 129 top: Vanessa Kuemmerle, Vee Horticulture; 130 bottom: Scott Brinitzer Design Associates; 132: Bud Stuckey; 133 top right: Scott Brinitzer Design Associates; 133 bottom: winecountrycoops.com; 134–135: Kelly Bowman Greenwood; 136–137: Katey Mulligan, Liquidambar Garden Design; 140: Scott Brinitzer Design Associates; 141 top left: Scott Brinitzer Design Associates; 141 bottom left: Lighting design by Outdoor Illumination; 141 right: Raymond Jungles, Inc.; 142 bottom right: James David; 143 top: Allsop Home and Garden; 143 bottom left: Scott Brinitzer Design Associates; 143 bottom right: Peter O. Whiteley; 144: Nick Williams & Associates (www.nickwilliamsdesigns.com); 145: Scott Brinitzer Design Associates; 146: PolyScapes Landscape Construction & Design; 147 top: Embellish, Katrina King; 147 middle: Jeffrey Gordon Smith Landscape Architecture; 150: Tony Gwilliam; John Greenlee; 151 top left: Peter O. Whiteley; 151 top right: Hillary Curtis, David Thorne Landscape Architects; 151 bottom: The Fockele Garden Company; containers by David McMullin, New Moon Gardens; 152 left: Nancy Goslee Power & Associates; 153 left: Sanchez & Maddux, Inc.; 154: Tina Beebe & Buzz Yudell; 155 top: Bud Stuckey; 156: Architecture: Dale Gardon Design; Interior Design: Tamm Jasper Interiors; 157 top: Reisinger Rigging; 157 bottom: Scott Brinitzer Design

Associates; **158:** Architecture: Folck West + Savage; Interior Design: Lovelace Interiors; **159 top:** Oehme, van Sweden & Associates; **159 bottom:** Scott Brinitzer Design Associates; **161:** John Cava Architect; **162–163:** Ken Coverdell, Blue Sky Designs, Inc.; **164–165:** Jim Pollack Design; **167:** Vermeil Design; **168:** Robert Glazier, Hill Glazier Architects and Andrew Glazier, Wild West Gardens; **169 top left:** Sydney Eddison; **169 top right:** Scott Brinitzer Design Associates; **169 bottom:** Clinton & Associates; **170 top right:** James David; **171 top:** Luis Llenza Garden Design; **171 bottom right:** Living Green; **172:** Raymond Jungles, Inc.; **173 top left:** Vanessa Kuemmerle, Vee Horticulture; **173 top right:** The Sweetwater Cabana; Beach House Style; **177 middle and bottom:** Scott Brinitzer Design Associates;

178 top right: Jeffrey Gordon Smith Landscape Architecture; **178 bottom left:** James David; **178 bottom right:** Anne Sheldon; **179:** Ron Benoit Associates; **180:** Cevan Forristt Design; **181 top left:** Peter O. Whiteley, **181 bottom left:** Vanessa Kuemmerle, Vee Horticulture, **181 right:** Jim and Paula Umbeck; **182 top left:** James David; **182 bottom left:** Scott Brinitzer Design Associates; **183 top:** Shirley Alexandra Watts Garden Design and Installation; **183 bottom:** Allen Landscaping; **184–185:** Rob Pressman; **189:** Cherry Burton; **191 bottom right:** Derviss + Chavez Design + Build; **192 middle:** Floribunda Landworks; **193:** Clinton & Associates; **194:** Scott Brinitzer Design Associates; **195 top:** The Fockele Garden Company; **195 bottom:** Hillary Curtis, David Thorne Landscape Architects; **196 top:**

Michael Keller; **196 middle and bottom:** Kathryn Rogers, Sogno Design Group; **197:** Architect: Lee H. Skolnick; **198:** Scott Brinitzer Design Associates; **199 top:** Architect: Mark Hutker Associates & Architects, Inc.; Landscape Architect: Steve Stimson Associates; **200:** Lane Williams, builder; **201:** Jon Carloftis; **202–203:** Craig Bergmann, **205:** Richard Wm. Wogisch, **206:** Vanessa Kuemmerle, Vee Horticulture; **208:** P.O.P.S. Landscaping; **210:** Scott Brinitzer Design Associates; **212:** Lisa Stamm; **213:** Freeland Tanner; **214:** Lighting design by Outdoor Illumination; **215 top:** Luis Llenza Garden Design; **215 bottom:** Chris Jocobson, GardenArt Group; **216:** Tom Mannion Landscape Design; **218:** Kelly Bowman Greenwood; **219:** Suzanne Porter; **221:** James David.

Special Thanks

We would like to thank the designers, architects, and builders who contributed to this book, and the homeowners who graciously allowed us to photograph their backyards. Kimberley Burch, Bill Stephens, and Spencer Toy of Sunset deserve a huge thank you for their help in coordinating the photography. Special thanks to Ben Marks of Sunset Books, Sally Reilly of Time Inc., and Paul Bay, Craig Birmingham, Steve Davis, Pete Pierce, Jeff Steinke, and Gary Worth of Punch! for making the included design software a reality.

Index

DVD System Requirements

PC Products

- Intel®, Pentium®, Celeron®, Xeon® and Centrino or AMD®, Athlon®, Duron and Opteron Processor
- Windows® 98 or higher
- 64 MB of RAM
- 1.5 GB of hard disk space
- VGA video card displaying at least 1024 × 768 with 24-bit color (32-bit, if available)
- DVD-ROM Drive
- Mouse or other pointing device
- 32 MB minimum video card memory

Macintosh Products

- PowerPC G3 or higher, Intel Core Solo or higher
- OS X 10.4 or higher
- 128 MB of RAM
- 1.5 GB of hard disk space
- VGA video card displaying at least 1024 × 768 resolution using millions of colors
- DVD-ROM Drive
- Mouse or other pointing device
- 32 MB minimum video card memory